Branding the Man

Why Men Are the Next Frontier in Fashion Retail

‖‖‖

by Bertrand Pellegrin

Allworth
Press

12 11 10 09   5 4 3 2 1

The Talented Mr. Ripley by Patricia Highsmith is © 1993 Diogenes Verlag AG Zurich.

Published by Allworth Press
An imprint of Allworth Communications
10 East 23rd Street, New York, NY 10010

Jacket and interior designs by Tamara Gildengers Connolly
Page composition/typography by Integra Software Services, Pvt., Ltd., Pondicherry, India

ISBN: 978-1-58115-663-8

Library of Congress Cataloging-in-Publication Data:
Pellegrin, Bertrand.
Branding the man : why men are the next frontier in fashion retail / by Bertrand Pellegrin.
    p. cm.
Includes bibliographical references and index.
ISBN 978-1-58115-663-8 (alk. paper)
1. Male consumers.   2. Marketing.   3. Fashion.   I. Title.
HC79.C6P45 2009
746.9'20688—dc22
                                    2009014852
Printed in the United States of America

To my father.

"Evenings looking at his clothes—his clothes and Dickie's—and feeling Dickie's rings between his palms, and running his fingers over the antelope suitcase he had bought at Gucci's. He had polished the suitcase with a special English leather dressing, not that it needed polishing because he took such good care of it, but for its protection. He loved possessions, not masses of them, but a select few that he did not part with. They gave a man self-respect. Not ostentation but quality, and the love that cherished the quality. Possessions reminded him that he existed, and made him enjoy his existence. It was simple as that. And wasn't that worth something? He existed."

— *from* The Talented Mr. Ripley *(1955) by Patricia Highsmith*

Table of Contents

Acknowledgments

This book began as a master's thesis at the Academy of Art University. I knew then that this would become part of a larger project, but it took several years of shuttling between two continents before I was able to gain the additional insight I needed to understand the evolving American man.

Long ago, when I was a student at Lewis and Clark College, I became fascinated with the behavioral differences in gender and how a society reinforces those behaviors through a range of socialized messages and ritualized behavior. The politics of appearance not only affirm those messages but also enforce the gender uniform—the clothes we wear to convey our places amongst one another, as men or as women. One's appearance can guarantee social acceptance and disguise social class; it ensures that the status quo, as it relates to gender behavior, is maintained. Appearance is but one way we express who we are, but it is also how we interpret who someone else is.

As a brand strategist and retail consultant, I use a variety of tools and extensive research to study the politics of appearance, whether in San Francisco or Seoul. But it is the people—friends, colleagues, mentors, teachers, and family—who have been my most valuable allies and experts in helping make this book a provocative and useful tool for those who are interested in its subject.

So, it is with tremendous gratitude and appreciation that I acknowledge those from long ago and yesterday who gave me their patience and wisdom: at Lewis and Clark College, Professors Robert Goldman and Deborah Heath, and at the Academy of Art University, Joan Bergholt and retail consultants Jim Warshell and Gail Gordon (my earliest advisors in the development of the project thesis).

It was in Korea, China, and Hong Kong that I began much of my initial comparative research on how people shop and gained insight on the complex world of luxury retailing. I must thank Hyun Ouk Cho, CEO of LVMH Korea, Ltd.; Jean Yang, former retail manager of Louis Vuitton Korea, Ltd.; and Ms. Sunyoon Chang, former executive director of Lotte Shopping Group's Avenuel department store, in particular for her trust and and belief in my vision for a new approach to Korean luxury department stores.

Thanks must also go to my generous experts in the U.S. fashion industry: David Pilnick, senior vice president of international business ventures for Saks Fifth Avenue; designer John Varvatos; Mickey Drexler, CEO, and Todd Snyder, senior vice president of menswear at J.Crew: John MacDowell, owner of Oslo's men's store in Seattle; Ken Lombardi, director of marketing, and Maz Hattori, buying manager, at Lombardi Sports in San Francisco; Marshal Cohen and Beth Boyle at NPD Research, Inc., who provided contextual analysis and research; and Andrew Hargadon, associate professor of technology management at the Graduate School of Management at University of California, Davis.

Special thanks must also be given to Dr. Kit Yarrow, consumer psychologist at Golden Gate University, for her compelling insight and research on the next generation of male consumers; and to my friend and mentor, Wilkes Bashford, president and CEO of Wilkes Bashford Stores, for sharing his wisdom in running one of the country's best men's stores and for allowing me to use his store window and staff for the cover of the book.

To Yao-Lien Wang for his unfailing support and friendship. He not only designed the charts and graphs but also designed the initial manuscript when it was a humble master's thesis. He has never ceased to open my eyes to the world of design and art and has always encouraged me to express my ideas. Thank you also to Teru Yoshida, photographer of the image used on the book jacket as well as the portraits of men on the streets of U.S. cities.

To my publisher, Tad Crawford, and my editor, Janet Robbins, for their generous patience and sage advice in the revisions and additions to the final manuscript.

Last, I would like to thank my mother, Dr. Helen Pellegrin, who made exhaustive edits to this manuscript and was instrumental in shaping the delivery of what was said and how.

None of this book would be possible without these fine people, and I humbly offer my indebted thanks. It is with great honor and respect that I share my success with each of them.

Introduction

This book is the result of several years of reflection, observation, and practice in the field of retail marketing and branding with special emphasis on the male customer. In the course of my experience, I have reached certain conclusions about the psychological, aesthetic, and practical aspects of turning men from passive acquirers into enthusiastic, loyal—even, dare I say, fashionable—buyers.

I propose to discuss how and why men shop and how a store can make itself irresistible to the masculine mind by appealing to perhaps unconscious desires. In addition, I will suggest methods that can be used to help store employees become valuable assets rather than grudging participants.

Branding the Man does not pretend to be the definitive manual about selling to men, nor are its recommendations to be taken as gospel. Rather, I see it as a study of a fast-developing population and the art of marketing to it. I hope it will be useful to neophytes (entrepreneurs and investors who are exploring the potential of the men's retail market); thought-provoking to seasoned merchandisers and retail managers; and ultimately entertaining and provocative to anyone who has ever wondered what on earth men see and feel when they enter a store.

In this book, I explore the remarkable and intriguing ways men have changed in the decades since the 1950s: the politics, social upheavals, and sociological underpinnings that have made the American man an even more attractive and susceptible market for everything from household products, to food, to fashion. Fashion is very much a pivotal marketing opportunity because fashion is inextricably part of the "lifestyle" of consumers' self-expression, and in turn leads to other areas of consumption such as fine dining, travel, cars, and private aircrafts.

In other words, men have evolved in how they see themselves, and they continue to do so. This has resulted in a sea change in the men's retail market. In his groundbreaking book *Ways of Seeing*, author John Berger writes of the innate "sense of being" possessed by men and women. The book, first published in 1972 at the height of the American feminist movement, reflects the sexual politics that were then at a boiling point. But it is also insightful in the way it describes the politics of appearances. Writes Berger:

> *Men act and women appear. Men look at women. Women watch themselves being looked at. This determines not only most relations between men and women but also the relations of women to themselves. The surveyor of woman in herself is male: the surveyed female. Thus she turns herself into an object—and most particularly, an object of vision: a sight.*[1]

It's the kind of theory that made total sense—at the time.

But now fast forward to another time and another century (this one), when a great deal has changed in the spectrum of

Man, the Calvin Klein fragrance, is just one example of how retailers attempt to speak to the men's market—not terribly successfully or imaginatively. A fragrance name like this only underscores the fact that men are still unclear on how to comfortably identify themselves.

social norms. Where once women were the object and men the surveyors (and appraisers) of their appearance, the playing field has become just as political for men—but now men are also a spectacle to everyone, including themselves.

Some might blame it on the "gay revolution," claiming that gay culture has made narcissism ubiquitous in both sexes. Consider that by the 1980s, the influence of gay style had worked its way into the mainstream. An advertisement for Calvin Klein cologne, for instance, featured a smooth-skinned, muscular man who stared desirously into his own eyes reflected in a mirror, his lips only a short distance from a kiss. Back then, few straight men would ever have admitted to finding

this advertisement appealing. Around the same time, fashion critic Holly Brubach pronounced Giorgio Armani's suits
"decidedly homosexual" in style.[2] Since then, however, men's
vanity (if that is what it is) and self-awareness have progressed
at warp speed and the narcissism once ascribed solely to women
(and of course, homosexuals) is but a distant memory. Fences
have fallen, and the evolution of acceptable appearance has
opened the door allowing men to display their inner peacock
more openly. The questions now become, how can the market
best entice this new, emerging male into the store, and once
inside, will he buy?

What was once considered emblematic of vanity is now
considered merely good grooming. The act of enhancing one's
personal appearance has a purpose beyond that of simply
attracting the opposite sex; in fact, career experts are almost
unanimous in saying that a man's appearance is increasingly
important in his getting a job. Youth, vitality, and virility—
packaged with a seemingly effortless stylishness—all contribute
to creating an aura of invincibility that can convince onlookers
of a man's potential to slay dragons in the business world. One
need only observe the exponential increase in the use of hair
color, plastic surgery,[3] and gym memberships to be aware of the
existence of an untapped male market. Gym culture alone has
become a booming area of male transformation. Here, male
vanity is a legitimate heterosexual trait (it's about health, after
all—right?). Cultural critic Jonathan Rauch calls it the "buff
revolution," pointing out that since the 1980s, men's bodies
have become just as fetishized as women's, with magazines,
advertising, television, and film showcasing the toned, polished
man of today.[4]

But being a man in America is not easy. Men perform for one another; it is, writes Michael Kimmel, a "homosocial experience: performed for, and judged by, other men." It is a performance that clearly demonstrates, *I'm not gay*. This, argues Kimmel, is "the single cardinal rule of manhood, the one from which all the other characteristics—wealth, power, status, strength, physicality—are derived."[5] With this in mind, it is easy to see why the men's store is still a confusing place for men to affirm their sense of masculinity or, for that matter, to discover an enhanced vision of themselves.

Retailers, buyers, and marketers continue to miss the mark when it comes to how they sell to straight men. Despite a slow and steady sartorial evolution of the species, one thing hasn't changed: the store. Here is the very place where men should be able to satisfy their aspirations, yet by and large it has stagnated. While trendy boutique brands like Zara, H&M, and Abercrombie & Fitch frantically cater to the whims of the millennial (thirteen- to twenty-four-year-old) female shopper with a disposable income, the world of men's retail has remained a kind of fly in amber, frozen in time with the same century-old style of merchandising and selling. Whether located in a department store or in a mid level chain boutique, menswear is often the problem area, with store managers shifting product around in a desperate attempt to galvanize that part of the store.

Mainstream retailers like Macy's, Nordstrom, and Neiman Marcus are still practicing the same antiquated selling techniques they used for the better part of the twentieth century. Their efforts at being hip—which typically involve scattering a few pieces of modern furniture, adding plasma screen TVs, and blasting pop music—ring false. In many department

The BRAVO television program, *Queer Eye for the Straight Guy* broke new ground in profiling straight men's lifestyle quandaries, answering them in a straightforward and entertaining manner that highlighted the mainstream belief that gay men are somehow more fashion savvy.

stores, just *getting* to the men's department can be a challenge, and often requires a trek through the winding aisles of the cosmetics departments. Once he arrives, the male shopper is greeted by the usual landscape: acres of ties, suits, and shirts—with, in addition, the overtly trendy stuff most guys don't know how or where to wear. So what's missing here? In the first place, stores should not simply present clothes the way a hardware store lays out tools, paint, and gadgets. It should provide education and guidance for the man who is hungry for something more than the usual "blue plate special" of khakis and polo shirts—if he could only figure out what that might be. Additionally, a 2003 NPD Group study has shown that more men pick out their own clothing now than ever before. Only three years earlier, the same study showed that women were still making men's shopping decisions. The gap is getting increasingly smaller as men begin to make their own purchasing decisions without the help of women. Obviously, department stores should be positioning themselves as helpers, not as obstacles.

Men are now foraging for themselves, consulting each other or one of the newly revamped men's fashion and lifestyle magazines like *Men's Fitness* (which used to be about, well, fitness, but now also covers fashion). What was once a decidedly "gay" preoccupation is now becoming an acceptable—and even necessary—way for a man to express his identity. The gay man has gradually—and at times imperceptibly—but very definitely influenced the straight man.

So what's taking the U.S. market so long to catch up? Chalk it up to a distinctly American reluctance to appear preoccupied with one's looks (lest we appear too gay, too intellectual, or too European) combined with the notion that "dressing up" reeks of elitism. It is the antithesis of the image the "regular guy" holds dear: honest, unpretentious, and uninfluenced by convention or etiquette.

But that's changing. For the die-hard "regular guy," the modern world of today is fast developing new expectations. As the social and business worlds become more competitive, the politics of appearance become more complicated. Men are discovering the value of their inner peacock in accessing the upper echelons of the business world and the inner sanctums of the elite. Now, everyone wants to have arrived (without, hopefully, appearing to be an *arriviste*).

First, though, let's take a look at the evolving man before we follow him into the store. What makes a guy buy, and why?

A Note Regarding Target Market

For the purposes of this book, the target market is an American male between twenty-four and forty-five years of age and who identifies himself as straight. This is an upwardly mobile consumer who has had some exposure to fashion and is becoming aware of the meaning of "quality" and "style." Branding specialist Marc Gobé calls those in this demographic "eXcels," an allusion to the mostly defunct term, "Generation X." Gobé estimates that there are approximately 44 million eXcels in the United States and that outside of the Baby Boomer and Generation "Y" demographics (also known as "millennials," or those born between 1982 and 1994), they are perhaps the most significant target market. In the words of one analyst, "They have a sharp and discriminating taste, which freely adapts and subverts existing fashions and brands while meeting hip fashions and individualizing [themselves]. In other words, your basic postmodern portrait."

By their late twenties, men in this market are foregoing their teenage style of dressing for something a little more grown up. They experiment with trendy and high fashion merchandise. The majority of market research currently available focuses primarily on the eighteen- to thirty-four-year-old demographic. However, at the time of this writing, market analysts are segmenting men into smaller and more precise market demographics, which will provide even more accuracy for the analysis of consumer behavior.

CHAPTER ONE
Who's The Man?

The man of today is a work in progress. If it were possible to flip through every example of popular culture produced during the last hundred years—movies, magazines, advertising—we would observe the snail's pace at which male style has evolved. Silhouettes get wider and slimmer (and back again), and collars and ties expand and retract, but for the most part, the elements of style are the same.

The political and social revolutions of the '60s and '70s opened the door to change. Today, men's fashion is less about the fleeting trends of Nehru jackets or bell-bottoms than it is about the awakening of a man's self-expression and self-creation. It is the growing desire to transcend the traditional components of the traditional wardrobe and emerge as unique.

Men are aware—now more than ever—that appearance can satisfy more than just vanity; it can convey an array of social messages, including status, class, profession, and sexual confidence. In much the same way that clothes and makeup allow a woman to transform herself, men have come to discover the silent language of appearance and the power it can wield in the workplace, with women, and even with each other. While still wary of appearing dandyish or effeminate, the evolving man realizes that "style" can propel him into higher spheres, both professionally and personally.

The Search for Self: Style and Culture

In 1958, historian Arthur Schlesinger, Jr., wrote in *Esquire* that men are alarmingly uncertain of their identity as men. He pondered:

> *What has happened to the American male? For a long time he seemed utterly confident in his manhood, sure of his masculine role in society, easy and definite in his sense of sexual identity. Today men are more and more conscious of maleness not as a fact but as a problem. The ways by which American men affirm their masculinity are uncertain and obscure. There are multiplying signs, indeed, that something has gone badly wrong with the American male's conception of himself.*[1]

For many years, sociologists have been fascinated by the modern world's effect on social identity. In Erving Goffman's book, *Behavior in Public Places: Notes on the Social Organization of Gatherings* (1963), he writes, "we assume a certain face or social identity that others help us to maintain."[2] For men, in particular, this means that at an early age they are indoctrinated with a list of expectations that they are expected to fulfill in order to be "manly"—especially terms of behavior and appearance. As they mature, the larger society continues to remind them of these expectations. In subsequent research, sociologist Herbert Marcuse elaborated on Goffman's findings and developed what he termed "self-schemas," or beliefs in oneself that guide the processing of "self-relevant information."[3] In other words, men often make decisions based on the expectations of the society in which they live, and behave accordingly. While men often pretend to be unaware of their own style, they know, as does everyone else, that style is one of the most important ways of reading who (or what) a person is. Men sometimes use clothes to subtly communicate what they hope will be interpreted as masculinity.

Sociologist Stuart Ewen likens style to "the most common realm of our society, in which the need for a better way of life is acknowledged on a material level." We demonstrate who we are via possessions—clothes, accessories, cars, and so on-that reveal our status politically, sexually, and in terms of class. Ewen continues, "Style is a device of conformity, or opposition. Style conveys mood. Style is a device by which we judge—and are judged by—others. It is worn on the surface of our bodies.... To 'have a lot of style' is an accolade of remarkable personhood."[4] Later research by sociologists Hazel Markus and Paula Nurius shows that individuals consider their actions not only in relation to their "current selves, but their possible selves as well—what they might become, would like to become, and are afraid of becoming in the future."[5] Anthropologist Sophie Woodward, in writing about the importance of sportswear items like hoodies, trainers, and tracksuits, says such clothes "have become ubiquitous as part of the uniform of youth—yet the functionality or practicality of sportswear is only one concern people have when choosing to dress this way, for sportswear forms part of the everyday performance of identity, staged not on playing fields but in the streets, clubs, and bars of the city."[6] Appearances are very much a performance, and we see now that the power of menswear retail resides in its potential to tap into this awareness and need for self-identity and social performance.

Interestingly, this contrasts sharply with men in certain other non-Western cultures where self-perception is less of an act of individualism and more collectivist in nature, especially in countries like Japan, China, and Korea. Indeed, elsewhere in the world, the sartorial symbols of masculinity are remarkably different. As the world gets smaller, global cultures become more influential and may perhaps even foreshadow what is to come for the American man.

"Public self-consciousness" is the idea that while individuals focus on their own inner thoughts and feelings, they are also keenly aware of how others see them. Within just the past twenty years, men have even more overtly crossed over into a world—hitherto assigned to women—where appearances are vital. As John Berger asserted in 1972, "men act and women appear," but today's men must do both. And in many cases, they're more than willing to.

Marketing to the Post-Boomer Man

Who is he? Generally speaking, he was born after the mid-1960s and came of age in the 1980s. These are men who grew up in the aftermath of the feminist movement and discovered more choices in how they chose to define themselves. These choices did not free them from the constraints of manhood's traditional social mores, but they certainly loosened the reins.[7] Today, young men born in the 1980s are even more free to experiment with their appearance, and in many ways are even more willing to do so. The phrase, "real men don't eat quiche" (coined in the book of the same name in 1982), was meant as a humorous reaction to the postfeminist man.

Today's guy is evolving into what I call the "New American Dandy"; he wants to have his quiche and eat it too. That means he still wants to chill with the guys in a bar, but he also wants to dress up, go to a cocktail lounge, and meet a girl. He still dreams of the day he'll have his dream car and maybe finally get a Patek Philippe or Rolex watch. Aesthetics have become just as important as function (performance); men have learned that, while a new cell phone or computer can make you look cool, so can a good suit. Thanks to men's lifestyle magazines like *Maxim* or *Stuff,* "bespoke" has entered his vocabulary. One industry analyst summarized it:

> *I call it the new "youth customer." He's in his thirties, but he still wants to be sexy and get laid. He's been educated about jeans, thanks to denim gurus like Diesel, but now he's decided that if he's going to spend $200 on jeans, he wants to trade up on the rest of his look as well.*[8]

Nowhere is the phenomenon of the evolving male customer more visible than within the 18–34 demographic. "Young men are the new generation of consumers," says Candace Corlett, a partner with WSL Strategic Retail. "They shop for clothing more like women than they do like older men, and are becoming pretty passionate shoppers."[9] A glance at a broad range of studies over the past ten years reveals a volatile men's market with peaks and valleys not unlike those in women's retail. For instance, a joint study by market research firms KSA and NPD showed that while overall retail sales of menswear dropped in 2001, they actually increased for the 18–34 demographic,

Music producer Pharrell Williams is a classic example of a younger generation that revels in what could be called the "New American Dandy": a man who is self-assured and comfortable dressing to impress.

COURTESY LVMH

going up 2.5 percent to $9.2 billion. Interestingly, of all the groups surveyed, this demographic was still the only one to spend more—not less—on clothing.[10] The same study in 2002 showed even more detail:

- Younger men make 3.6 shopping trips a week, compared to the 4.1 made by younger women

- Younger men visit an average of 1.6 stores on each trip, nearly as many as are visited by younger women (1.9)

- 29 percent of these men report that they are shopping more in malls than they did a year ago, well above the 18 percent of younger women who do

- 22 percent of men 18–34 shop more in department stores, compared to a mere 16 percent of younger women[11]

Marketing to the Masses:
How *Men's Health* Defines a Growing Demographic

Men are more preoccupied with their physical appearance than ever before. The success of men's magazines like *Men's Health* certainly indicates as much. *Men's Health* bills itself as a magazine that "speaks to every aspect of a man's life, providing its readers with the latest information on health, fitness, fashion, nutrition, relationships, travel, and money."[15] (If you shut your eyes, you'd swear you were listening to a description of *Cosmopolitan*.) Interestingly, a category percentage breakdown of topics in twelve issues reveals that 12 percent are on relationships—that's after "Food and Nutrition" (15 percent) and "Fitness for Beauty" (16 percent).

It stands to reason that the magazine has found a growing audience. The average reader of *Men's Health* is single, 37.5 years of age, and college educated, with an average income of $67,218.[12] That's a man with money to burn and a battle of the bulge to fight. It's also someone who is learning that if clothes indeed make the man, the body can make the clothes mean so much more. Minutely detailed lessons in creating a more attractive appearance can be found in every issue.

The magazine's rise in readership is well documented in the pages of industry quarterlies, an incredible success when you consider not only the downward spiral of magazine profits in general, but the formidable competition: *Esquire, Playboy, GQ, Rolling Stone, Men's Journal, Maxim,* and *Men's Fitness*. But all of these magazines still wrestle with how to talk about fashion without coming off as girly. *Cargo,* the magazine that hoped to be the men's version of *Lucky,* barely made it off the ground in 2004 and fizzled in less than two years. Is it that men aren't ready to shop with a magazine, or does doing so require too much imagination? One consultant on the *Cargo* project felt confident that men were more than ready for a shopping

magazine of their own. "Men shop differently [from] women, but they still use media as a source of information."[13] If only. The truth is, a magazine simply isn't enough to reinforce a man's confidence when it comes to making purchase decisions. Men are less likely to turn to a magazine to tell them how to shop and more likely to rely on proven results and the testimony of people they trust. A magazine like *Cargo* wholeheartedly embraced pure fashion; its tone was somewhere between neutered and feminine. Jimmy Jellinek, the editor of *Stuff* magazine, says of the male consumer, "Shopping is about using possessions as a means to augment power."[14] And that's precisely why stores still matter when it comes to selling to men: because they offer an opportunity to deliver a distinct voice and point of view, along with the customer service to back it up. In the end, a magazine does not invite interaction; rather, it dictates. A store has the potential to engage the customer with a customized and immersive experience.

The study goes on to suggest that "men are marrying later in life and shopping for their own apartments without female help. When they do marry, they are active participants in the selections that go into the bridal registry. Stores see couples more than moms and daughters at the registry." In other words, men are becoming active participants in realms that were previously "female."

While overall retail sales have been challenged the past few years by a struggling American economy, menswear hasn't exactly faired poorly. In April and May of 2008, sales of men's clothing rose 2 percent from a year earlier, compared with a 2.8 percent decline in women's wear. High-end specialty stores showed particular growth, with a 3-percent increase in only twelve months.[15] Still, department stores struggle with the men's category (a situation we'll explore further, later in this book.)

The statistics reflect that the hunter/gatherer model (in which men hunt and women gather) is fast becoming an antiquated notion of how men shop. Of course, such figures pertain largely to the urban male in major American cities rather than those elsewhere in the United States. The statistics cited above also serve to illustrate an interesting shopping trend that has trickled down to other demographics. Across the board, the male consumer is changing. They are upwardly mobile and established professionals who are enticed by trends in cars and technology, and are now ready now for the clothes that go with them. They are also generally followers, not leaders, and rely on the advice of close friends—male or female—to guide them in their decisions. And they keenly observe the ease with which celebrities like Brad Pitt or George Clooney exhibit confidence with knife-sharp suits, hand-made watches, and a rakish tilt to their fedoras.

Brad Pitt and George Clooney are the first modern movie stars to make fashion a distinctive part of their identities, and they have done so without compromising their masculinity. Each has brought a greater awareness of style to the mainstream.

Celebrity Style and Social Class

Indeed, cultural critics point to stars like Pitt and Clooney as being instrumental in influencing men and claim that they even helped reposition the staid business suit into its place in the new fashion lexicon. Pamela Church Gibson, senior lecturer in cultural studies at the London College of Fashion, writes: "Cinematic icons, on and off screen, reflect current bewilderment and the need for reassurance together with a wish for fashion leaders whose style makes some clear statement about the particular form of masculinity they embody.... In clubs, pubs, and bars, it is possible to see just how many young, white men have adopted this particular look."[16] In much the same way, Justin Timberlake, Usher, and numerous other young pop stars remain influential as style icons, acting both as billboards and instructors for the mainstream populace. In *The Social Agenda of Clothing*, critic Diane Crane asserts: "Clothes in the workplace mark social hierarchies very precisely. Leisure clothing, by contrast, tends to blur social class differences. Rich and poor participate in the same stylistic world, which is dominated by images from popular culture and the entertainment media."[17] In the United States especially, people have become increasingly casual to the point that "dressing up" is a sign of distinction. And with the pop culture mirror showing so many celebrity peacocks, men are willing to give it a try. According to a Unit Marketing study, in 2007, about 10 percent of U.S. luxury consumers bought men's formal eveningwear—up from 7 percent in 2006. Did it help that Sean "P. Diddy" Combs, David Beckham, and Usher were recently seen superbly decked out in custom eveningwear? Probably.

If one travels to the smaller cities of America, like Memphis, Fort Lauderdale, Grand Rapids, or Kansas City, one discovers that even "the rest of the guys" are co-opting the look of the moment. Even mall retailers like H&M and J.Crew are pushing

PHOTO COURTESY AMC.

The AMC series *Mad Men* glorifies an era when the American male most closely identified with the appurtenances of maculine appearance. Nothing defined manhood more than the suit and tie. Today, the television program has given a new generation of men an appreciation for classic tailoring.

formalwear. The men in suburban America have already adopted the look of a sport coat with jeans and a black dress shirt, and (thankfully) left the fleece vest at home on a dinner out with their girlfriends. These are men who yearn to look effortlessly cool, grown-up but without the attitude, like the guys on the HBO series *Entourage*. The vintage rocker tee paired with the pinstriped blazer says, "I'm not with the band—I'm *in* the band." In fact, leisurewear has come to democratize fashion to the point where both rich and poor take part in the same stylistic world, thanks in large part to pop culture and the media, which have broadcast a sartorial style that knows no boundaries. The suit, ever the aspirational symbol of having "arrived" into the world of wealth and success, has been similarly reappropriated. It continues to be the ultimate, bullet-proof symbol of the masculine world of power—and renewed interest has only been furthered by popular shows like AMC's *Mad Men*.

I'm Not Gay, I'm Metrosexual

It was in 2001 that the mainstream media caught on to a term originally coined by a British journalist to describe this burgeoning demographic. The term "metrosexual" applies to any heterosexual urban male who has learned to appreciate the merits of good grooming and dressing. But what began as a pop culture quirk has now grown into a full-on marketing phenomenon, with research groups and merchandisers struggling to keep up.[18] A man in his late twenties to mid-thirties is now willing to buy Bruno Magli shoes, $50 face creams, and custom-tailored shirts, once he understands how they can demonstrably improve his appearance, and is reassured by the fact that "important" people such as celebrities are also indulging in such items.

Marian Salzman, executive vice president and chief strategy officer at Euro RSCG, who was in charge of the initial primary marketing research on so-called metrosexual men, says, "They are the style-makers. It doesn't mean your average Joe American is going to copy everything they do ... but unless you study these guys, you don't know where Joe American is heading." The mass media have been a key tool in selling the "new" man, with countless TV programs in which hosts, anchors, actors, and yes, even Ordinary Joes are walking billboards for the fashions of today. Says Patrick Robinson, former designer for Perry Ellis and current Gap, Inc., creative director : "Friends of mine who are rap stars and movie stars were always the scruffy ones, and now, suddenly, they want to be dressed up."[22]

Sean Combs is an exaggerated example of the trend, but he's also helped spark a revolution in the way the hip-hop world has evolved. Since he launched his own clothing line, hip-hop fashion is no longer about velour tracksuits and gold chains. *New Yorker* writer Michael Specter accompanied Combs on a trip to Paris for fashion week. He notes:

> *There were several garment racks in the living room, with more than a dozen suits, scores of shirts, leather jackets, what appeared to be 20 or so belts, and twice as many ties. There were enough shoes to last a lifetime, and enough sneakers to outfit the Knicks. Versace had provided some of the clothes, but most had been flown over from New York. "Can you possibly wear all this in four days?" I asked Combs. "All I can do is try," he replied with a wink.[23]*

Taming the Beast:
Why Men's Grooming Profits Continue to Rise

There is a growing interest in what the men's cosmetics industry cautiously describes as "self-care." A spa in Utah, for instance, reports that 35 percent of their clients are men. Nickel, a French men-only spa, has opened salons in New York and San Francisco. Let's not forget, too, the men's market for bath and shower products that has increased exponentially to profits well over $20 million every year.

Manufacturers are watching as men explore the benefits (real or imagined) of beauty and grooming products. A walk down the aisles of pharmacies and department store cosmetics departments reveals a host of new products geared towards men's face care, including aftershaves, deodorants, and depilatories. In fact, more and more men are shaving, trimming, and waxing away hair, such that Nair, the hair removal lotion for women, has launched a silver-bottled version for men. When Procter & Gamble decided to reposition its Old Spice brand as "Old Spice High Endurance" (like with so many men's grooming products, the name is vaguely sexual), it did so with a Web site that featured a woman in a bikini with the tagline: "When she sweats, it's sexy. When you sweat, you stink." [19]

More and more men are enjoying spa treatments like facials and pedicures—but they're doing it privately, and in places that don't feature candles and flowers. The International Spa Association recently estimated that 31 percent of spa-goers are men. The "man spa" offers plenty of privacy (some provide screens between chairs so men don't actually have to look at each other) and amenities such as flat-screen TVs with plenty of sports channels. Bikini Cuts in Salt Lake

4VOO is a Canadian brand of men's cosmetics that claims its customer is "the man who is a leader in everything that he does, and understands that his grooming, and appearance are vital to his professional and personal success." Extreme? Perhaps. But men are increasingly experimenting with "enhanced" skincare products.

City gives Hooters a run for its money with its bevy of young women providing manicures—while wearing bikinis. Most importantly, the name of the treatment should sound "manly." Said one spa owner, "Men are results-oriented. Call it a 'foot repair' and guys know what the result will be." [20]

But there are a growing number of men who prefer to take care of hair removal themselves. In 2007, Philips launched the "Bodygroom," the first device to officially target all male hair "beneath the chin, including those sensitive spots below the belt." [21] One can only imagine the terrible accidents that happened to the men who chose wet razors to groom themselves in places that demand deft use of a hand mirror. Philips launched a wildly successful Web campaign that featured a man in a white bathrobe extolling the virtues of his newly smooth, er, groin, but rather than show his groin, they flashed images of nuts, carrots, etc., with the claim that all that hair removal from the southern region adds an extra "optical inch" to that ... carrot.

It is both striking and significant that a man who is such an influential figure in the world of hip-hop and pop culture can be so whole-heartedly attuned to fashion. As a result, Combs's Sean John line has become a Seventh Avenue hit, showcasing clothes that carefully straddle the line between so-called urban street looks and a swanky, gangster-style flair.

But what happens with Sean Combs is, of course, not indicative of what is happening with all men. Michael Kimmel, in his book, *Guyland: The Perilous World Where Men Become Boys,* writes that men are in fact delaying adulthood—which certainly seems to account for so many middle-aged men still wearing baseball caps, slouchy jeans, and other clothes more indicative of a teenager than of a grown man. "Passage between

COURTESY SEAN COMBS FRAGRANCES

Sean Combs was the first hip-hop star to dramatically evolve "ghetto fabulous" into a more sophisticated look that had all the earmarks of classic American elegance. He continues to follow in the footsteps of Ralph Lauren in creating a fashion empire that is distinctly "to the manor born."

adolescence and adulthood has morphed from a transitional moment to a separate life stage," writes Kimmel. "Adolescence starts earlier and earlier, and adulthood starts later and later."[24] One hardly needs to point out that this fact makes it harder and harder to lure American men into a store. For retailers, it means an even more dedicated approach to coaching men in the elements of style and more efficiency in balancing store selection with equal parts casualwear and tailoring. Those who can teach their customers the finer points in merging styles, colors, and textures will go far in broadening the value of their offer in a men's ever-evolving lifestyles.

Chapter 1: The Take-Away

Men are more aware than ever that having personal style is important. They now know that they are judged by subtle codes of appearance and that these codes influence their potential to move within professional and social circles—not to mention the impressions they can make on the opposite sex. Statistics show that the eighteen- to thirty-five-year-old male consumer is becoming a force to be reckoned with, but retailers are still stumbling in how to respond to him. Popular culture continues to make a considerable impact on men's fashion, with film and sports celebrities leading the way in marketing fashion merchandise like suits and luxury goods that were previously more the domain of the white-collar worker and leisure class. Fashion retail as we know it is on the verge of changing—but only if retailers take the time to understand the male customer.

CHAPTER TWO
Why the Men's Store Must Change

We might ask why retailers still struggle to market menswear if, in fact, men are so obviously seeking much of what women seek: the power of self-identity, the thrill of looking good on the world "stage." According to Paco Underhill, "the manufacturers, retailers, and display designers who pay attention to male ways, who are willing to adapt the shopping experience to [men], will have an edge in the twenty-first century." He continues, "all aspects of business are going to have to anticipate how men's social roles will change, and the future is going to belong to whoever gets there first."[1] Nevertheless, men continue to be either disregarded or misunderstood in the retail environment. They are the invisible shopper, wandering about in a world that has been created largely for women. The market hasn't invested in this customer and underestimates their power as consumers.

What's the problem? Surely not a lack of great merchandise. Rather it's a lack of great positioning, marketing, and service. It's a lack of meaningful, authentic messaging similar to that which has been used on women for ages. However, there are certainly differences: unlike women, men don't necessarily want to see every color a shirt comes in. They just need someone to

tell them which one to buy. Barry Schwartz, psychology professor at Swarthmore College, says the problem with retailers
today is that there is an "explosion of choice," leaving consumers
even more uncertain than before about their purchase decisions.
The result is "doubt over a good choice and misery over a bad
one," with some not buying at all.[2] Schwartz makes a case for
"good enough," whereby choice is limited to which item suits
one's needs best. The question then becomes, if men can't find
what they're looking for, and often don't even know *what* they're
looking for, where's the opportunity? That answer might lie in
creating the perfect environment where they can discover both.

Consider the classic gentleman's store of yore: Brooks
Brothers, Abercrombie & Fitch (before it became a destination for teenage hunks and babes), and others frequented by
our fathers and grandfathers. These stores were branded by

For many, Brooks Brothers is still the classic menswear destination. While the brand
recently refreshed its retail format, it is still more or less typical of the "gentleman's club"
style of men's stores.

the honesty of their names, the consistency of their products, and the integrity of their service. In turn, they branded their customers. In its heyday, referring to a man as "very Brooks Brothers" was a kind of blue-blood shorthand for Ivy League and Wall Street. Brooks Brothers was "dad:" traditional, secure, and dependable. The clothes, indeed, made the man.

In the 1970s, when menswear began to take some creative leaps, it was a handful of designers who kept the selling floor vibrant and exciting. Allan Ellinger, of Marketing Management Group, says that what they did was revolutionary. "Pierre Cardin started [a revolution] in 1972 with an entirely new silhouette," adding that others, such as Yves Saint Laurent, Giorgio Armani, and Calvin Klein, also offered unique interpretations of suits and a distinct "lifestyle" approach to how they marketed their looks. In fact, it was really the first time that anyone actually used the term "lifestyle" in the context of a fashion brand. Wilkes Bashford, the veteran San Francisco specialty retailer with a 28,000 square foot emporium carrying the finest in menswear, only underscores that point. "We were the first to carry Versace, Armani, and Claude Montana," says Bashford. "This was around 1974 until the 1980s. Our slogan then was 'menswear for the bold conservative.' People came to us because they knew they would find something extremely modern. Suddenly fashion became fashion for men, with actual trends. It wasn't about the subtle changes of lapels or cuffs on pants, but it was about real fashion that changed from season to season in dramatic ways."[3] Bashford began his business in 1966 and has since opened three other stores in California, each carrying the top names in men's tailored clothing: Kiton, Armani, and Brioni, among others. His business plan: sell with conviction and authority. That strategy has done well for the Wilkes Bashford brand, even in the worst of times when men's casual wear threatened to nearly annihilate tailored menswear.

The breakdown in office hierarchical structures and a changing workforce meant a less formal way of dressing, and that meant a more casual way of dressing for work. By the mid-1970s, the necktie suffered its largest decline in decades. By the 1990s, men had stocked up on so much casualwear—khakis and polo shirts—that there was little left to sell them. It seemed men had completely forgotten how to dress for business, let alone how to dress with personal style. The situation became serious enough in the spring of 2000 that *Time* magazine proclaimed in a headline, "The Suit is Dead: Bankers Dressing Like Internet Executives Create the Biggest Threat to the Suit in 100 Years. Can It Survive?"[4] But with the dot-com bust came a silver lining. The search for new jobs required a return

Men's Wearhouse is one of the largest and most successful purveyors of basic suits for the young professional. Its strategic retail locations give it direct access to its core customer.

to tradition, and with the demise of "casual Fridays" (which had by then become "casual Mondays, Tuesdays, Wednesdays …") there came a resurgence in tailored menswear.

These days, dressing for work in something other than jeans or khakis has become much more the norm in American companies, and this has given the U.S. menswear market a huge boost. By 2002, sales of menswear began to increase, and in June of 2003, that middle-brow mecca of bargain suits, Men's Wearhouse, showed comparable sales of 7.6 percent. By 2006, the store saw same-store sales jump 8.1 percent. Meanwhile, JoS. A Banks Clothiers Inc.—a national chain with 318 stores—climbed to 15.2 percent[5] in the same period, and by 2006, soared to 20.7 percent. You'd think an economic downturn would change all that, but it didn't. According to NPD Group, in the first quarter of 2007, when unemployment hovered at 5 percent, menswear sales rose 0.8 percent in the first quarter of 2007 while women's wear sales fell 3.5 percent. In just three months during that period, menswear sales jumped 2.3 percent while women's dropped 3 percent.

Nevertheless, challenges still lie ahead for the menswear business, and nowhere is this more visible than in department stores. Abbey Doneger, president of the Doneger Research Group, said that there is hope—but first there must be change. "There are plenty of positive things happening out there amid the negative," he says. "It's just that there's got to be a point of differentiation and a reason for being. You've got to offer the customer that value equation—a combination of selection, price, and quality. Some stores do it well and others don't." Indeed, despite a roller-coaster economy, menswear sales have shown a growing trend in potential sales.

Macy's men's store in San Francisco. The company still struggles with understanding how to communicate to such a diverse customer base, which perhaps explains this visual merchandising decision.

Department stores, for so long a women's favorite, still struggle to entice customers into their men's departments. Efforts to jazz up the men's department rarely seem to help. The suit area with its dark, knotty woods and brass chandeliers is often jarringly juxtaposed with glacially modern "designer" sections full of trendy clothes that are anathema to men: white jeans, flowered shirts, and anything with a lot of straps or zippers. Once upon a time, department store shopping was a calm, routine experience featuring white-haired salesmen with measuring tapes. Now it is a confusing mess of merchandise that borders on schizophrenic. Just who is the customer? The Ordinary Joe who shops today is confronted by a range of looks that may or may not align themselves with his sense of self in an atmosphere that is often intimidating and overwhelming.

Merchandisers—men and women who are usually well ahead of the fashion curve and make the buying decisions for stores—are perpetually hopeful that the latest buys from the boldest new designers will fly off the shelves. All too often they don't. When I was marketing director for a major luxury department store, the fashion director and buyers would return from Milan or Paris certain that something completely improbable like white hot pants or satin bowed shirts (yes, for men) would be the season's biggest sellers. The truth is, many fashion executives are ultimately buying the merchandise for themselves and have little to no sense of who their real male customer is. Maybe 2 percent of their customers—the hard-core fashionistas—will actually buy some of this stuff. Targeting a specific customer profile is one thing, but alienating the majority is another, and when a department store tries too hard the result affects the bottom line.

Here's the dilemma: how does a store reach out to the regular guy who is searching for his sartorial self? If we know that a man's identity and self-perception at, say, eighteen, twenty-four, and thirty-five change as the decades pass, how can we brand this man and demystify his search for style? Consider that sales research indicates that a thirty-year-old man will often buy the same pants as a forty-five-year-old man. Not what retailers want to hear, but perhaps the larger issues are, why are we denying the truth about how men shop, and why is it that retail strategy is still bogged down in cliché and stereotype?

One obvious reason is clichéd thinking. Supposedly, men react in one of or a combination of the following ways: (1) they "grab and go"; (2) they "whine and wait"; and (3) they feel that shopping environments are too uncomfortably "feminine."

In fact, none of these are consistently true of men's shopping perceptions and behaviors. Indeed, as we have seen in chapter one, it appears that men have transcended their outdated gender role and actually have the potential to enjoy shopping as much as women do.

In fact, I would argue that the issue is less about the product and more about customer service, store design, and the way the total shopping experience impacts and reinforces a man's desire to return to the store again and again. In other words, what else does the customer get from the experience besides the product itself? In point of fact, this is the fundamental key to great branding: the customer is buying a product, yes, but he is doing so in a place of significance, and he is buying the goods not merely out of need but in order to be associated with the place and its brand. In essence, he is buying style, because "style" is a passport to another realm—one of class and association (what sociologist Stuart Ewen calls, "the visual grammar of our lives"). Style constitutes a politics of change—even if only on the surface of our lives. As Ewen observes, "It is a behavioral model that is closely interwoven with modern patterns of survival and desire." If the male customer understands the need for style—that what is offered will provide a quantifiable change to his life—he will buy. The key, then, is to create the right combination of ambiance, service, and merchandise to make that happen. The stage once set, the atmosphere once established, the result is almost predictable: he will buy. And, under such conditions, he will return ... again and again.

The responsibility, then, comes down to the store itself, be it a brick-and-mortar retail environment or an online presence.

A great men's store should be like your best friend or big brother, or the movie star whose style you'd like to emulate. You trust his taste and respect his choices. A great men's store should be both friend and mentor. Such a store should be a "meta-store," offering an experience beyond the purchase. Strategist Marc Gobé suggests that branding is not so much about market share but "is really always about mind and emotions share."[5] I would go further and posit that branding the man comes down to a holistic approach to menswear retailing, focusing firmly on a richly textured experience that offers both the tangible and intangible. The customer discovers style in a place that simultaneously entertains and enlightens and that gives him a sense of community and self-confidence. When he leaves, it is with a feeling of having been understood and valued. Will he want to return? In all probability, yes. Can a men's store really cast such a seductive spell? Read on.

Chapter 2: The Take-Away

The men's store has more or less remained unchanged for the better part of the last century. But in the 1970s, social and political movements helped usher in new silhouettes and designs, and men became receptive to new perspectives in men's fashion. New designers like Pierre Cardin, Versace, and Armani challenged norms in men's businesswear. By the 1990s, the workplace had become so casual that retailers struggled with finding more to sell to them than polo shirts and khakis. But by 2002, men began tiring of the casual Friday look, and suddenly, the suit was back. With a struggling economy comes the need for men to repossess the classic symbols of masculine power. But where a store might succeed in stocking the right goods, they can still miss the mark in offering a hospitable store environment. Understanding what men value in their purchase experiences becomes more and more critical to remaining competitive in the market.

CHAPTER THREE
When Retail is Relevant

The definition of value as it pertains to the purchase experience has changed. Value for money has become as much about quality as it is about price. For instance, in one study, 60 percent of shoppers said they were willing to pay more for higher-quality clothing rather than sacrifice quality for price. A surprising 65 percent said quality was more important even than style. Of these shoppers, 18.3 percent were men—the fastest-growing group in the retail clothing market. Who are these men? They're twenty-five to fifty-five years old, and 59 percent of them (compared to 41 percent of women) make quality-driven apparel purchases.[1]

These numbers are not very different from research provided by Cotton Incorporated. 72 percent of men say price is the most important piece of information they consider when purchasing a garment, while 70 percent say they would rather choose apparel that is higher in quality over more fashionable goods. So it makes sense to extrapolate from these facts and to deduce that as men become more accustomed to and educated about fashion, they will value style as much as they currently value quality. Durand Guion, fashion director for Macy's West, agrees. "More men today have had to adopt a better standard of dressing," he says. "It is now a requirement to be accepted into certain clubs, impress the opposite sex, or climb the corporate ladder. There will always be a segment of the male population who [wants] nothing to do with style or fashion, but it is clearly becoming a smaller percentage."[2]

In short, men's requirements are evolving into those similar to the female customer's—demanding style, quality, and value (price). More important, they are also becoming consumers who are sensitive to intangible value and are open to perceiving that an object can have a value beyond its price tag. This is the appeal of any number of luxury brands such as Burberry or Louis Vuitton.

Clothing, like everything else, has come to signify status and lifestyle. It is no secret that designers today are infusing their brands with the same kind of symbolic power as has traditionally been used in the marketing of perfume. A woman might not be able to afford a Chanel suit, but she can afford a bottle of Chanel No. 5. This brand strategy has become standard practice with virtually everything, especially in the domain of luxury retailers. Ralph Lauren long ago set the standard for this aspirational, lifestyle approach to marketing a branded experience. In addition to all his other products, he now has restaurants. Armani has hotels. Hermès has helicopters. You name it, we brand it. In other words, why sell them the cow when you can sell them the whole farm?

Selling Aesthetics: When the Brand Becomes You

Remember that what luxury brands do so well is marketing a dream—a fantasy that lends an added value to the product the customer is buying. Men as much as women are susceptible to the imaginary status and emotional well-being that a product can appear to offer. That illusion is furthered by a complex set of values that reinforce the meaning of an object. Identity Management specialists Bernd Schmitt and Alex Simonson coined the phrase "marketing aesthetics" to describe how the use of sensory experiences communicates a brand's identity. Virtually every modern brand in the market today uses aesthetics to bring a more intense, emotional experience to the brand story. Brands with extensive heritage are well suited to using marketing aesthetics to enhance their product value.

Schmitt and Simonson argue a marketing approach (*Figure 1*) that establishes the attributes and benefits of

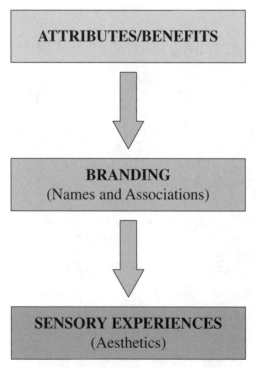

Figure 1. Focus of Marketing Approaches (Schmitt and Simonson)

a particular product—say, a men's tailored suit in Italian wool—and the branding that furthers its value with distinct connotations. A Brioni suit, for instance, is handmade in Italy and has been worn by every actor who has ever played James Bond (Sean Connery most notably). The final feature is the sensory experience that is associated with that product. These are the aesthetics that further enhance the brand's value and deliver an immersive experience for the customer: the store, the tailor who measures him for the suit, and the story of the brand, told in signage, symbol, and imagery. Together, these create a series of touch points that elevate the brand and further imbue the product (in this case, a suit) with an elevated significance and power. Writes brand strategist David Aaker,

Actor Sean Connery as James Bond still captures the imagination of men as the archetypal male. Wearing a Brioni suit doesn't hurt much either.

PHOTO COURTESY MGM

"A strong symbol can provide cohesion and structure to an identity and make it much easier to gain recognition and recall. Its presence can be a key ingredient of brand development and its absence can be a substantial handicap. Elevating symbols to the status of being part of the identity reflects their potential powers."[3]

World Retailing Strategies: Innovators in Experiential Retailing

It's important to note that some of the most innovative strategies in branded experiences and marketing aesthetics aren't happening in the United States. In Europe as well as in Asia, one finds a more receptive and sophisticated consumer fashion market, which, in turn, influences that of the United States.

London has been the epicenter of a merchandising and marketing approach that moves quickly in response to cultural trends. Nowhere is this more visible than at Topshop and Selfridges. Topshop's successful men's store, Topman, bills itself as "credible product at affordable prices for the young lad, ranging from great casual gear to the more formal suit." They call their store a "destination" where customers can go to relax, meet each other, and "most importantly, create their own unique [looks]." Topman aptly describes its customer as a "pubber, a clubber, a sports fan, and ladies man." He seeks fashion that "makes him feel comfortable and confident within himself and acceptable to his mates."[7] A visit to the store reveals a kind of male amusement park. The multilevel Oxford Circus shop is a wild blend of music, colored lights, fashion shows, and lounges bustling with attractive young men and women. On any given Saturday, there might be a live rock band, fashion show, or product demonstration. There is even a barbershop, a cafeteria, and a lounge. In other words, Topman has created an immersive environment where men are invited to stay and are given ample reason to do so (for more on immersive retailing, see chapter 10). The women's Topshop is located right next door, making it easy for one to drop off one's partner—or for that matter, find one. While Topman skews young, it still offers some interesting insights into "entertailing" for men.

Until recently, Selfridges, the venerable department store founded in 1909, appeared on the verge of collapse under the weight of its stodgy name and customer base. But after pouring $66.4 million into a state-of-the-art architectural vision (inspired by a Paco Rabanne chain-mail dress), it appears Selfridges could be on the rebound, having become very much a destination. The brand's most recent venture is a high-gloss, high-impact store that opened in 2003 to great fanfare. The 250,000-square-foot store in Birmingham is being ballyhooed as the new model for department store retailing; one expert even went so far as to say that the store had returned to the department store model of a century ago, adding that it was "great theatre."[4] There one can find bicycles, a tattoo salon, a bookshop, and fourteen restaurants—each tailored to the adjacent department's customer—creating an environment that makes shopping an interactive spectacle in which you, the customer, play the starring role. Chief architect Martin Illingwood, anxious not to have his design undone by overzealous brand directors, gave explicit guidelines for the way each brand was to be displayed.

PHOTO COURTESY ALFRED DUNHILL, LTD.

Alfred Dunhill, Ltd. has spent years attempting to recapture its reputation as the ultimate English gentleman's store. It has recently managed to excite a new generation with a younger, more approachable image that is still distinctly high-end.

Dunhill, Ltd., another old and well-known retailer, has rebranded itself as the kind of place where James Bond would shop, kitting out its stores with a tongue-in-cheek yet old-world charm that simultaneously removes any hint of its grandfatherly past. In 2008, Dunhill unveiled Bourdon House in London's Mayfair district. Housed in the former Georgian manor of the Duke of Westminster, the shop operates as a kind of brand theatre: it has all the right program elements to showcase Dunhill's newly polished image. A members-only club features a restaurant with resident sommelier, a bar, and luxury bedrooms (one presumes not of the by-the-day variety). For the general public, there is of course, a store, featuring Dunhill's latest creations from creative director Kim Jones. Consistent with the trend in men's grooming, Dunhill has also installed a classic barbershop and a spa.[5] After years of trying to dust off the brand, it looks like Dunhill has finally managed to distance itself from grandpa's pipe.

Just on the other side of the Channel is Colette, the furiously trendy Parisian boutique that has spawned imitators and developed fans around the world. It is so self-consciously chic and avant-garde as to be nearly nauseating, yet it is captivating. It was Colette that, in 1998, originated the concept of combining clothes with other goods: books, jewelry, cosmetics, art, food, and limited edition designer pieces created exclusively for the store. But because of its clubby atmosphere, not everyone is confident enough to walk in. This über-chic arrogance only adds to its cachet, of course, and has in turn made Colette an example of what's hot and what's not. One magazine gushes that Colette is a "store as editor, picking the hottest stuff from the hottest new designers and presenting it in a techno-style space."[6] Colette offers all the items one needs to feel completely beautiful and very "now": the sleek, severe clothing that one wears while listening to tragically hip music in a sparsely

PHOTO COURTESY OF COLETTE

The Colette store in Paris. Colette was the first to create the idea of a store as "curated exhibition," and over the years has become the arbiter of cool. More recently, the brand created a New York pop-up store in collaboration with Gap.

furnished flat (decorated with raw, vaguely pornographic books and other hopelessly decadent items).

Such is the store's influence that Gap—yes, Gap—came calling, and in 2008, Colette agreed to install a pop-up store concept in Gap's New York flagship. Gap, in its desperation to be hip again, had interestingly decided that a shot of cool from Colette would answer at least some of its problems. As of this writing, that remains to be seen. But what we do know is that Colette's magic touch with a branded retail environment, predicated on a "curated" experience, is precisely what so many brands are craving—especially in America. In other words, Colette is about a lifestyle, and the people who shop there buy one or all of the goods on display in order to feel they have arrived—ahead of the rest, *naturellement.*

Also in Paris, department stores are getting in step. Printemps, another classic department store (part of French conglomerate PPR) opened Printemps Homme in 2000. The seven-floor store features a private label as well as designer label fashions, with one floor dedicated to the sort of customer who might very well shop at Colette. Here you'll find club fly-ers, and a live deejay. You can also get a facial or manicure at the Nickel spa (for men only). Four floors up, you can have a cocktail in the lounge. While Printemps is still a department store, each of its floors' discrete boutiques (not unlike LA's Fred Segal) manages to feel very intimate.

The "Colette effect" has spread globally. Many different brands have adopted it, with varying degrees of success. In 2003, Dolce&Gabbana opened its first store devoted exclusively to men in an 18,000-square-foot palazzo in Milan. D&G created a decadent retail experience in an atmosphere redolent of the old-world gentleman's club (Hello, Ralph Lauren?). There is yet another sexy bar, an authentically Sicilian barbershop, and a grooming spa. The designers spent millions to make sure the customer comes, stays, and buys.

In Asia, the men's market has paved the way for trends in both the United States and throughout Europe. Tokyo, Seoul, Shanghai, and Hong Kong are each home to thriving men's retail markets that have grown by leaps and bounds. In these cities, vanity and class are critical commodities that enable a move up the socioeconomic ladder, and fashion is as much a tool as it is a pastime. In Japan, there is a far greater emphasis on the analysis of street fashion and the use of "quick response" (the merchandising strategy whereby order response and replenishment time is reduced in order to ensure that goods are available to meet inventory demand) to get the right merchandise onto store shelves. The men's clothing market in Japan grows exponentially every year and is currently hovering around $6 billion. In the early 1990s, it was the Japanese who drove the market for vintage and so-called premium denim. Magazines devoted to individual brands and even categories are many (Louis Vuitton, Gucci, Hermès—the list goes on). Fashion is a serious enough pastime there that some brands even go so far as to create Japan-exclusive product lines—not to mention building iconic flagship stores.

While not all of these brand strategies necessarily apply to men's retail, it is worth noting their aggressive approaches to understanding their target customers and designing highly detailed environments with a host of products and services that are specifically attuned to their lifestyles. In the next chapter, we'll look at some non-menswear environments that manage to do this, too, and whose success is that men stay and pay.

Chapter 3: The Take-Away

Men are becoming more like women in how they shop, and their demands are similarly on the basis of price, quality, and style. Intangible value is when an object is perceived as having greater value than its actual price. This value is the result of the range of characteristics and external and subconscious associations—celebrity endorsement, lifestyle, and other aspirational symbols—that increase the consumer's desire for the object. Marketing aesthetics (the marketing of sensory experiences in corporate or brand output that contributes to the organization's brand identity) ensures that this desire is further reinforced with other external symbols and signifiers that bring a heightened value to the product and the experience of purchasing the product. In the world of global retail, many brands have taken considerable steps to elevate the image of their goods with calculated and carefully programmed retail environments. In London, Selfridges has rebounded in the staid department store market with a circus-like atmosphere of activity and special services. In Paris, Colette continues to be the benchmark for the small, hip specialty store, so much so that even Gap tried to borrow some of its cool factor by installing a Colette pop-up store in its New York flagship. Meanwhile, European and Asian retailers continue to provide compelling case studies for the development of unique retail environments.

CHAPTER FOUR

Where the Boys Are

Historically, men have had men-only preserves that served to confirm their authority—a "man's world" where they could retreat from the noisy and annoying world of women and children. The gentleman's club, the hunting lodge—all are now gone or, at best, remain as quaint museum pieces most young men of another generation wouldn't enjoy anyway. Sociologist Michael Kimmel blames it on the "cultural feminization" of men and on the fact that there are few enclaves left that are truly "a man's world."[1] Whether one subscribes to this or not, it's a provocative idea in developing a men's environment.

Where does the man of today feel like a million dollars? Where does he experience the possibility for reward and achievement? Where is he relaxed enough to express himself and even spend some money? Here's a hint: it's not a men's clothing store. Interestingly, design and color scheme are not necessarily important factors. Unlike even the most successful stores, these environments don't need to try too hard—and that might just be why they work.

Bars, strip clubs, and electronics stores offer fascinating insight into the components of a place where men feel at ease. Unlike women, who are not only comfortable in stores but also in a variety of social environments and public spaces, men prefer to be among interactive distractions. They enjoy solitary distraction (watching sports on TV); group distraction (playing sports, drinking, and working out); and skilled distraction (video games, automobile repair, and home improvements). There are three important identifiers these places share:

1) **Environmental Factors** (they are functional and comfortable, according to certain standards of design and material)

2) **Social Activity Factors** (they offer casual and non-threatening interaction and are generally defined by some sort of activity)

3) **Gender Identity Factors** (they consistently reinforce and empower men's sense of manhood as defined by their culture and peers)

As you consider the following case studies, keep in mind how their various characteristics might be transferred to other retail opportunities. The accompanying diagrams will help you to understand the specific mechanics to their success.

"Where Everybody Knows Your Name": The Sports Bar

Much of the success of the classic television sitcom *Cheers* was certainly a result of its humor. However, its setting also played a role: as the theme song proclaims, Cheers is a place where "everybody knows your name." The show aired from 1982–1993 and received a record 111 Emmy nominations and twenty-six Emmy Awards. On its final night in May of 1993, fans gathered at sports bars around the country to bid it farewell.[2]

Men loved the show and it's no wonder why. The Cheers sports bar was the setting of a sentimental comedy that reminded guys of their college dormitory or fraternity house. This nostalgia may explain why, even today, men enjoy hanging out in sports bars in cities across the country. Despite certain stereotypes to the contrary, men are social beings—just not in the same way that women are. Men do enjoy doing things together; watching television in a lively environment with plenty of comfort food and beer is one of those things. It is a haphazard intimacy that works because it is instantly casual and nonthreatening. The successful sports bar (*Figure 2*) is typically dark, with wooden walls and floors. Usually, several televisions are on at once, tuned to sports or sports talk shows, and the mood is upbeat and unpretentious. The owner-bartender is often "one of the boys"—a necessity for any successful bar. This is a place that a man can easily visit alone and feel welcome. It's

A great sports bar is comfortable and entertaining and can deliver hours of entertainment for men, thanks to the booze, babes, and baseball.

Figure 2: The Sports Bar

not an elegant environment, but that's a big part of what makes men feel comfortable there—the sports bar is an extension of a den or frat house living room. Make a mess here and no one will know—or care.

Green's Sports Bar in San Francisco is a classic example. It has the important signifiers: walls cluttered with memorabilia, high school trophies, and lots of televisions (I counted thirteen). Television—more specifically, sports television—is a critical ingredient here. Network television has created a formula for giving men the ultimate satisfaction by reaffirming their intelligence and ability to discuss the finer points of a sporting event in a way that signals to those around them that they possess important "masculine" skills (logic and analysis). As Ava Rose and James Friedman note in their book *Out of Bounds*, it is the sports focus that provides the foundation to an experience of intense male bonding:

> *TV sports programs, in particular, position the audience as part of a fluid and ongoing dialogue inviting [them] to look, and look again, to interpret the image to respond to the emotional content of the spectacle and in a literal sense, to participate in the meta-discourse of sports. ... The television provides its viewers with access to a continuously evolving world, a community to which the sports fan can belong simply by tuning in ... the symbolic and actual community constructed by sports spectatorship in America is as masculine as the playing of the games themselves.*[3]

Green's Sports Bar is one such community, and the sports programs are a hearth around which the men gather for warmth and companionship. Together, the television and alcohol act as mediators and social matchmakers. Men debate the almost military strategy of a football game, but in essence they prove their value to and friendship for each other. That's important.

As the bartender told me, testosterone is what drives the energy of the bar experience. On any given night, men bark at the TVs and huddle over beers in almost artificially casual conversation. The bartender claims that men also love the memorabilia—even to the point of trying to buy it off the wall. Décor, while not elaborate, is a critical factor for a bar's success: it's unobtrusive, unchanging, and familiar. This is definitely an environment where men feel at home. One man described it as being "like walking into my mother's womb." Another said, "This place is my office." Still another mentioned that Green's is a good place to meet people, quickly adding, "… but I don't go to meet people, really."[4] This qualifier speaks to the essence of a sports bar: it's where men go to feel like men, and as is often the case, that feeling is unacknowledged, though it's palpably there. That unspoken character is precisely what makes a man's environment feel authentic. Author and scholar James B. Twitchell attributes the same quality to the baseball dugout. In *Where Men Hide*, he writes:

> *Like other places where only men congregate, the dugout is organized by unarticulated rules: who sits where, whose equipment goes where, and even what conversational topics are permissible are prescribed. As old-timer Waite Hoyt said, 'In the daytime you sat in the dugout and talked about women. At night you went out with women and talked about baseball.' … But some topics are taboo … the key to dugout etiquette is the same thing that makes it such a powerful force for men: this is a world without women, a world in which the masculine principle of bonding is never to be violated. You may chatter together, you joke together, you spit together, and from time to time, you charge the pitcher together. Woe to the player, even the multimillionaire player, who decides to sit it out and play the pacifist. The dugout makes that unthinkable.*[5]

What is clear, then, is that men seek friendship, solace, and refuge in places that help to reinforce their masculinity. Sports are inextricably linked to the sacred oath of loyalty, team spirit, and that distinctly American sentimentality for the love of the game.

Toys to Men: The Electronics Store

The electronics store is one of the best examples of great men's retailing (*Figure 3*). Stores like Best Buy are packed on any given weekend with men pushing buttons and reading product specifications. Like the sports bar, it is not a highly designed environment; it's all fluorescent lighting, basic shelving and countertops, and the cacophony of televisions, but men are generally oblivious to this aesthetic wasteland. This environment is about man and machine; here, customers can explore the miracles of modern technology and glory in their genius in mastering them. They can marvel at the power that lies within

Electronics stores continue to be one of men's favorite destinations, a place where they can enjoy the power of control and new technology.

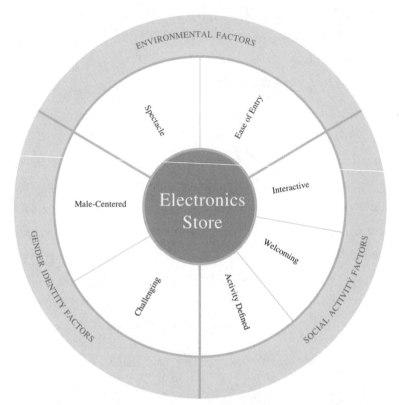

Figure 3: The Electronics Store

a piece of electronic equipment. The purchase happens when they've decided that without it, they will be hopelessly outdated and irrelevant in the multimedia world and that of their peers. Like an expensive watch, technology speaks to the modern man who wants to embrace the marvels of engineering.

Best Buy stores have an almost theme-park feel, with a maze of aisles that lead the shopper deeper and deeper into the vortex of increasingly expensive electronics. On a recent weekend, the home entertainment department was enjoying robust sales in plasma televisions, while Shania Twain sang her heart out from one of the gigantic displays. Nearby, a group of men watched a football game on a long bank of screens. Several guys were explaining appliances' features to their girlfriends with great seriousness. In a review of customer service among several electronics retailers, the *Wall Street Journal* cited Best Buy's success in customer service. The male newspaper reporter received thirty-seven minutes of undivided attention from the employee, who gave comprehensive and easy-to-understand product specifications and benefits.[6] Like so many men who work in electronics stores, these are guys who know just how much difference surround-sound can make when you're watching the Super Bowl.

But it is the Apple store that continues to be the Holy Grail of great retail—and not just as an electronics store. They have created the ultimate play land where shoppers can interact with the products and easily watch other customers try out equipment—an important part of the experience because it essentially makes Apple's customers part of the display. It's a convincing performance that reveals how easy it is to use the product. Experts say other stores could certainly take a page from Apple. "I think a lot of retailers use what I call the 'kitchen sink' approach," says Chris Anderson, director of The Marketing Arm, a firm that has guided clients like Wal-Mart and Procter & Gamble. "Let's throw everything on the sales floor and we're bound to sell some of it. There's literally tons of stuff to walk through and sift through. At some point, you just throw up your hands and say, 'I'm exhausted. Let's get out of here.'"[7]

The retail design and product displays at the Apple store are so spare and clean that it is clear why men in particular enjoy being there. There are no claustrophobic aisles and no cluttered signage. The hero is the product, and by association, so is the customer. The triumph of the Apple store experience is that the guy who wanders in and tries out a new computer or iPod is

The Apple store has become the benchmark for nearly every kind of retail. The brand has created signature environments that are clean and easy to navigate, and encourage the idea that a store and brand can operate as a community.

PHOTO COURTESY OF APPLE, INC.

able to have an experience whereby he controls the product and simultaneously enhances his knowledge, skill, and self-image. He is as sleek and shiny and modern as the very thing he holds in his hand. "Apple's quest is to create the ultimate shopping experience," says NPD's Marshal Cohen. "It's a a place to shop, learn how to use the product, learn what you can buy to enhance yourself … and most importantly, it's a place to come to feel comfortable and bond with the brand. No pressure to purchase, just a wholesome learning and entertaining environment."[8]

You Give Me Fever: The Strip Club

It's estimated that 14 percent of American men visit strip clubs on a regular basis. Strip clubs (*Figure 4*) offer not only beautiful women, but fully masculine, testosterone-charged male camaraderie. By and large, this is a group activity, where guys can encourage one another to show their interest in a particular

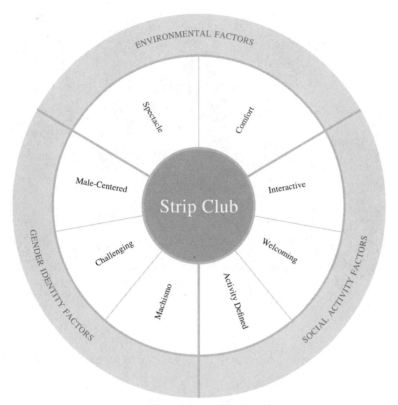

Figure 4: The Strip Club

woman and when the attention is returned (which, of course, it is—it's a business, after all), their masculine prowess is confirmed.

Like the sports bar, the strip club is an environment where men participate in an activity together. The overall mood is lighthearted and titillating. Anthropologist Katherine Frank has researched strip clubs extensively, both as a performer and as an ethnographer, and found that "the clubs provide an intermediate space—not work, not home—where men can enjoyably experience their bodies and selves through conversation, fantasy, and ritualized voyeurism."[9] The range of clubs varies from "classy" to "dive," but ultimately the reality is the same.

Strip clubs clearly offer titillation, but they also provide a place where men can be together and thus reinforce their identity as men. Women, far from secondary, allow men a kind of ritualized seduction.

This is an environment that is warm, inviting, and sexy. It makes men feel powerful and in charge of their desires while knowing full well that nothing will ever really happen. In his book, *Where Men Hide*, author James Twitchell says strip clubs help to reinforce men's need for community with each other:

> *The showgirl doesn't evoke the more complex interactions of reality ... 'Look, but don't touch' is not so much the showgirl's prohibition as it is a relief to the male viewer. So while the strip club may look like a brothel, its meaning is almost entirely to the contrary. Many men may go to a strip club because they can predict safe distance from women, because they know they can be macho without having to be sexual, because they know that now, at last, they can relate to—whew!—other men.*[10]

When Sex Sells: Study Shows Men Really Do Get Hot, Bothered … and Shop

It hardly comes as a surprise that a woman in a bikini can increase a man's sexual appetite. A men's spa in Salt Lake City, for instance, goes so far as to require its female employees to wear bikinis while servicing men with pedicures, manicures, and facials. But Belgian researchers Bram Van den Bergh, Siegfried DeWitte, and Luk Warlop explored the possibility that bikinis cause men to completely lose touch with the future, think only of immediate gratification, and in many cases make hasty judgments when it comes to rationalizing the importance of a long-term reward. To some, this will probably not be surprising, but the study offers fascinating insight on the how some individuals, when presented with a sensitive reward system, are incredibly susceptible to the effects of sex cues. The research study, titled "Bikinis Instigate Generalized Impatience in Intertemporal Choice" (*Journal of Consumer Research,* 2007), suggests that "exposure to sexual cues may affect decisions such as whether to purchase a less expensive item that can be enjoyed now or to save for a more expensive one."[13]

In the study, male subjects were exposed to specific sex cues: they were shown videos of women in bikinis or they were given bras to handle. In a reward system including soda pop, candy bars, and money, each were rendered equal and their significance and value fluctuated simply by virtue of the sense of urgency caused by the sex cues.

Tom Ford didn't need to do research to figure out how to sell his new men's fragrance.

"The results suggest that an induced sexual appetite instigates a greater urgency to consume *anything* rewarding."[14] In other words, the activation of sexual desires influences other brain systems involved in reward-seeking behavior—even the desire for money. Hand a man a bra to fondle and suddenly the reward—money or a candy bar—becomes considerably less important. The opportunity to engage in a fantasy about a beautiful woman is such that a man will often give way to impulsive behavior, even sacrificing the chances to increase a future reward (to gain more money later rather than right now). We know that sex sells, and it's easy to see why beautiful women continue to be the most successful marketing tool for the automobile and alcohol market. Is it any wonder that auto shows make sure that there are attractive women lounging on the hoods of the cars on display?

The Hungry I in San Francisco (not to be confused with the famous nightclub, now long gone) offers topless pole acts and lap dances. A source I spoke with said the majority of men who visit the Hungry I come in groups, and in general, those who come alone are looking for companionship, not just titillation. A dancer named "Marlene" says, "Titty bars are where guys can come and act like little boys." The men I saw were mostly in groups, encouraging each other to drink, meet girls, and "let loose."[11] It's not uncommon for one guy in the group to play the role of ringleader, goading the men who are shy. The goal, of course, is to see if the stripper might actually like you—and not just because you put some money in her G-string. Writes Thomas Beller in an article for *Men's Health*, "The idea that the stripper actually likes you is a delusion I've veered precariously near on a few occasions. Alcohol abets it a great deal. Most men become sentimental and romantic when they get drunk … with just a little wishful thinking, you grow convinced that the naked woman onstage thinks you are attractive and wants to talk to you." This illusion is precisely what makes the strip club environment a success. Here, men feel special and unique, potential winners in the sweepstakes of male sexuality. It is, as the author realizes, an irony that never loses its appeal. Writes Beller, "It's the last men's club. This place, where guys go for the explicit purpose of staring at long legs and naked breasts, is one of the few remaining places men can go to not think about women."[12]

Lookin' Good: The Social Vanity of Fitness Clubs

Fitness clubs (*Figure 5*) have become increasingly important to men who wish to enhance their appearance. Many men call it a "hobby," and visit as often as five or six days a week for up to two hours at a time. Research shows that, generally, men will give up another "big ticket" item before they give up their health club memberships. Weight training offers men the opportunity

Membership gyms like 24 Hour Fitness are equal parts public performance venue and laboratory where men can physically transform themselves. What was once a decidedly "gay" preoccupation has now become a ubiquitous part of a man's life.

to enhance their appearance without being labeled narcissistic. In her book *The Substance of Style*, Virginia Postrel writes, "As the stigma of being thought gay has diminished, paying attention to aesthetics has become less costly and more appealing for heterosexual men."[15]

Figure 5: The Gym or Fitness Club

The evolution of gym culture points to one very telling fact about how men have come to see themselves. As professor of sociology Michael Kimmel puts it, "The body did not *contain* the man, expressing the man within; now, that body *was* the man."[16] The body becomes instrumental in visually affirming the extent to which one is a man.

24 Hour Fitness is a one of the world's largest fitness chains. I visited one in San Francisco that, in an ingenious (although perhaps unintentional) stroke of great marketing, was located above a Circuit City electronics store. The atmosphere is minimal: steel floors, cement, and brightly painted walls. According

WHERE THE BOYS ARE

to a company source, this particular 24 Hour Fitness has an equal amount of male and female members, of which an estimated 75 percent are straight. Men generally come here to work out alone, critically scanning each muscle in the mirror. Some come in small groups of twos and threes, chatting between weight sets. Many men find this a convenient place to meet women, and I was told that women say they feel more comfortable meeting men here than in a bar.

Working out allows men to achieve a sense of control and self-enhancement that is not only socially permissible, but even reinforced by their peers. Writes Kimmel, "If masculinity cannot be achieved at work, perhaps it can be achieved by working out. Men's bodies provide another masculine testing ground. Millions of American men participate in the current health and fitness craze by dieting, jogging and bicycling, exercising, consuming health foods and various bottled waters, and purchasing high-end fitness equipment. 'Iron Man' triathlons push men beyond normal physical limits to explore the boundaries of the body."[17]

The refuge of the gym allows men to focus on themselves— and on one another—and to take part in a community of men who devote themselves to the mastery of physical enhancement.

Chapter 4: The Take-Away

While men might not always feel comfortable shopping in a store, there are other environments where men do feel comfortable. Historically, men always had places like hunting lodges and private clubs that served to reaffirm their hegemony and masculinity. In examining the scheme of places where men feel comfortable, it is intriguing to consider the role of sports bars, fitness gyms, electronics stores, and strip clubs. Each offers compelling evidence of the mechanics for what makes men feel comfortable and, in most cases, inclined to part with their money. Each offers a sense of community, and its interior design does not attempt to conceal its function. They are almost all defined by comfortable furnishings and noisy distraction and, in the case of strip clubs, sex.

CHAPTER FIVE

Where Men Are King

Historian Elisabeth Badinter, in her research on masculine identity, posits that while men are indeed evolving, there are still "imperatives," or foundations that form the basis of how men measure themselves: 1) Men must be men—"no sissy stuff"; 2) They must be competitive and able to constantly demonstrate their success (or potential for success) and superiority; 3) They must be "detached and impassive"; and 4) They must be willing to take risks and face danger.[1] With these points in mind, it becomes much clearer why the environments I've profiled fulfill one or more of these attributes and give insight on how to go about shaping the ideal environment for branding the man.

But these environments also reinforce what we already know about what sociologist Ray Oldenberg called "the third place": namely, that after the two primary anchors of home and workplace, people—all people—seek a third place in which they can facilitate and foster creative interaction.[2] Such places are largely informal and offer free or inexpensive food and drinks, are close to home or work, and are comfortably populated with friends and regular patrons. Howard Schultz, founder of Starbucks, wasted little time in capitalizing on the concept of the third place in developing his chain of coffee shops. Today, Starbucks is still the telecommuter's home away from home.

Like a sports bar, Starbucks offers the individual a place he or she can visit to work, daydream, find friendship, and most importantly, feel like part of a community. While a sports bar or electronics store, for instance, are not identical in form or function or in what they offer a male customer, one is able to see the overlap in the experience touchpoints and the critical design and service factors that entice and engage the customer in a specific environment.

While men characteristically feel at home in the worlds of work and physical activity, they are typically less comfortable in places that ask them to make decisions on how they dress themselves. Fashion retail presents the shopper with merchandise and we are given the choice to explore its potential to satisfy certain real or aspirational requirements: protection from the elements, an enhanced appearance, or the cultural code signals of status and success. This process of vanity and self-enhancement is arguably a female realm. While men are not exempt from this, the means by which it happens are usually secret and private, a half-guilty pleasure in discovering how best to advertise one's inner Adonis. The next generation of men—often referred to as Generation Y—is already on the cusp of being more confident in attending to their appearance, but the majority still rules: by and large, men are meant to deny that they are aware of their personal style instead seeking other ways of demonstrating who they are.

A women's clothing store, for instance, makes the quest for physical enhancement a delightful escape—it's fun. "Women really want a fantasy when they shop and they're much more susceptible to those triggers than men are," says consumer psychologist Kit Yarrow. "The store is a playground for women, but men are always wondering what they're supposed to be doing there. To navigate and explore such a place is like traveling to a foreign country. The biggest concession to men a store will make is to add some chairs for them to sit down."[3]

In chapter 4, we explored how bars, gyms, electronics stores, and strip clubs have core characteristics that not only offer proven value—their purpose and benefits are for the most part already demonstrated—but also serve as a promised reinforcement of male confidence and sense of self. But how do they do that? *Figure 6* breaks down the overlapping factors that together make these environments a quantifiable success in satisfying male needs and desires. We see that the environmental factors (comfort, spectacle, and ease of entry) are quite critical. In all of these environments, men can easily enter and establish themselves comfortably. They can find a focus for their attention that permits them to enjoy themselves in an essentially public space, with other people around them. Similarly, the social activity factors underscore that each of these spaces is nonthreatening and allows a man to interact with people, objects, or both. The casual conversation and tools of engagement (sports, electronics, fitness machines, or the simulated seduction of women) further allow men to demonstrate their expertise and perhaps even improve it. Meanwhile the gender identity factors serve to highlight their outwardly demonstrated male behavior. By virtue of just being there, a man is reaffirmed of his masculine identity because the environments are outwardly understood by society at large as "male centered." Here, machismo is not only acceptable but openly encouraged, with a range of tools to demonstrate men's expertise in traditional male challenges.

We now can understand that a male environment is less about the subtle and more about the overt and that ideally, it permits men to demonstrate their masculinity in a safe and semipublic space. Equally important is that it is demonstrated in plain view of other men, further confirming a man's membership in the world of men. These retail-oriented spaces (bars, electronics stores, gyms, and strip clubs) speak boldly of what they can and will offer the man who comes there. Says Yarrow, "Retail stores are, by and large, very 'designed'—I might even say over-designed—and they're really created to make the process of discovery a major part of the experience. Women really enjoy that discovery process; men find it not only confusing and intimidating but unnecessary. The environment where a man feels comfortable has a more or less singular focus, and the return value is immediate and clear."[4]

But that's changing as we speak. Yarrow, who, with *USA Today* journalist Jayne O'Donnell, has coauthored the book *Gen BuY: Why Teens, Tweens, and 20-Somethings Buy and How They're Revolutionizing Retail,* sees an implicit generational shift in how younger men are shaping their identities, and shopping is playing a big role in that. "These guys are roaming stores like Urban Outfitters and understanding the language of pop culture and how that's translated into personal style. There's a much bigger idea going on here of using clothes to send a message to a specific audience: maybe a certain peer social group, or girls—I mean, these are boys, after all."[5]

The environmental factors and experience touchpoints I've highlighted only underscore the cultural norms of gender roles. Women can, as a rule, easily find intimacy with friends, coworkers, or family members, whereas men traditionally struggle with meeting people outside of the workplace or their core groups of friends. For men, however, socialization

ENVIRONMENTAL FACTORS: Functional and Comfortable

Comfort	casual furniture, indirect lighting, "rugged and classic" style
	comfortably "classy": plush furnishings, wood finishes, soft/dim lighting.
	functional design, no-frills equipment and furniture
Spectacle	televised sports, table sports (pool, pinball, etc.)
	products are prominently displayed and switched on
	women perform; a "titillating" entry experience
	men and women do physical exercise in an open space
Ease of Entry	welcoming approach/exterior; open doors and windows.
	few obstacles, product categories clearly marked

SOCIAL ACTIVITY FACTORS: Casual and Non Threatening Community

Interactive	communication/intimacy mediated by televised sports
	customers are encouraged to engage with product
	customers encouraged to engage with performers
Welcoming	"be yourself" atmosphere
	"friendly" sales associates
	All men are equal
	"dressed down" environment allows for casual interaction
Activity Defined	televised sports demands participation (watching & discussing) and eases interaction
	technology as "reactive toy"
	drinking and paying for women's attention
	activity acts as social mediator in sharing equipment, assisting in reps, etc.

GENDER IDENTITY FACTORS: Empowers and Affirms Masculinity

Male-Centered	beer and sports, male kinship
	mastery of technology affirms men's ability in logic
	men are primary audience
	bodybuilding and fitness defines muscle and silhouette
Machismo	Sports arouses release of aggression/excitement
	expressions of interest/arousal
	men observe each other and themselves in mirrors
Challenging	test of skill with women, playful competition with other men
	test of skill and strength; passive-aggressive competition with other men

Figure 6: Breakdown of Male-Centered Environments

and traditional behavioral norms as prescribed by gender can often make it more complicated for men to find intimacy. Male-to-male communication and intimacy is typically facilitated by activities such as sports, drinking, home improvement tasks, and so on. Like women, men in the right environment will spend money, and when men feel good, they'll happily part with their money to make that feeling last. In the case of sports bars and strip clubs, the social exchange that comes with the cocktail only adds to the convivial atmosphere and the sense of belonging. In fact, the sports bar is an excellent example of an environment that possesses a lasting integrity when it comes to male social spaces. Sports bars do not masquerade as anything other than what they are. The atmosphere says, "be yourself," and men love it for that reason.

What we learn from the sports bar, electronics store, strip club, and gym is that these are environments with overlapping characteristics that are enticing and approachable. The men's store needs analogous attractions. Where the over-fifty-year-old man is comfortable with the classic men's store of yesterday, today's eighteen- to forty-five-year-old man is less so, and less comfortable with these traditional retail environments. A walk through any number of menswear departments and specialty stores—of all classes—exposes a distinct lack of innovation. Instead, these stores and departments betray a desperate attempt to satisfy too many customers, too many vendors, and ultimately, what one merchant summarized as "too much sameness." So how does a man find himself in a sea of sameness?

Each of the examples I've cited offers an insight into what a male customer looks for: belonging and companionship (the sports bar), entertainment and discovery (the electronics store), an enhanced physical self and self-confidence (the gym), and female attention and titillation (strip clubs.) Here are environments that offer intimacy without commitment; a sense of security; and an atmosphere where they can bond, engage, and feel certain of their position in the world as well as their power as men. Men perpetually seek activities and opportunities for self-expression that demonstrate—both to themselves and to the world at large—their manhood. The experience of engaging in watching sports, mastering technology, ogling women, or working out is part of a deeper need for men to participate in a prescribed set of activities. Says Yarrow, "The store environment needs to be re-calibrated for men so that men can participate in the discovery process of who they are and can become. A great store lets the customer do just that. But it's still a mystery for a lot of retailers of how to make it happen."[6]

In other words, a great men's retail store satisfies the psychosocial needs of men and proves it with the merchandise it sells. But can that experience happen for men with something as ubiquitous and mundane as purchasing a pair of jeans or a T-shirt? Yes, provided all the key elements are there. In the coming chapters, we'll examine the components necessary for creating an optimal men's retail experience.

Chapter 5: The Take-Away

The case studies of sports bar, electronics store, fitness gym, and strip club each illustrate the components necessary to designing the ideal men's environment—even a men's clothing store. Men seek belonging and companionship (the sports bar), entertainment (the electronics store), an enhanced physical self (the gym), and female attention and titillation (the

strip club.) A successful model of a men's retail store is predicated on the compatibility of merchandise and the authenticity
of the environment in which it is housed. The sports bar is
perhaps the most uniquely honest men's environment in that it
does not masquerade as anything other than what it is. A great
men's store asks only that you "be yourself." A male-oriented
environment is less about the subtle and more about the overt,
and ideally, permits men to demonstrate their masculinity in
a safe and semipublic space. Equally important is that it is
demonstrated in plain view of other men, further confirming a
man's membership in the world of men. These retail-oriented
spaces (bars, electronics stores, gyms, and strip clubs) speak
boldly of what they can and will offer the man who comes
there. What we learn from these spaces can be translated into
the components of a traditional men's clothing store.

CHAPTER SIX

Creating the Branded Men's Environment

When we hear the word "branding," we tend to think of the usual trademarks, logos, and taglines—that vast array of corporate icons that do battle for a customer's attention in a crowded marketplace of options. The integrity of a brand—any brand—is based upon the dialogue that goods or services create with the consumer on a visceral and more or less unconscious level. It is about creating an authentic experience that connects with the consumer through deeply personal, innovative products, services, and store experience. It is about making the brand uniquely specific to the consumer's culture and social concerns, to the point that it appears to extend its tentacles into multiple aspects of a person's life. John and Nicholas O'Shaughnessy, in their book, *The Marketing Power of Emotion*, observe: "Whatever the case may be, brand images can evoke emotional bonding with the customer, creating trust and arousing loyalty."[1] The brand is the crucial link between an essentially cold (and often redundant) product and a heightened emotional meaning targeting a specific audience. Audrey Balkind, CEO of Frankfurt Balkind, defines the goal of brand identity as "not just surface consistency but inner coherence."[2]

A successful brand is one that appears to offer the promise that it will perform according to the purchaser's wishes. It is not essential that the promise be of superior performance but rather that it suggest the enhancement of self-identity or some other intangible and highly desirable benefit. It is like the quintessential example of sublime marketing "Coke is Life," which pretty much seals the deal—what more remains to be said? Thus, a great brand is a rational exchange (needs-based, exchange of currency) but also a subconscious emotional exchange (desire-based). In other words, for the customer, its implied benefits outweigh its actual utility. It certainly works with women (cosmetics advertising notwithstanding), but can it be made to work for men? Emphatically, yes—provided all the key elements are there.

To create the optimal menswear environment is to create an authenticity—authenticity of store experience as well as of branded product that communicates an "authentic" message, which in turn fosters loyalty. Loyalty branding insures that each of the isolated components of the experience—store, service, merchandise, and so on—locks together into a seamless whole and resonates in a meaningful and authentic way with the customer. When this occurs, the sterile, linear purchase experience of product and purchase has been transcended. Everyone benefits.

The Evolving Male Customer

In studying sales figures, focus groups, and a broad range of data on shopping behavior, it is increasingly clear that men shop in a remarkably uniform pattern based not simply on social class but on a stage of social development—both personal and professional. Where once the politics of appearance centered on the meaning behind a woman's self-presentation, a similar statement can now apply to men. I've developed the Men's Style Cycle (*Figure 7*) in order to show how men's fashion needs and desires are actually a progression in three stages. It's important to note that, while American men are indeed evolving in their self-identity, the politics of appearance is still highly political when it applies to men. Societal norms continue to exert their power over how men perceive themselves, and how others perceive them. Anthropologist Sophie Woodward aptly says that identity "may be articulated through a desire for sameness, to 'fit in,' and for differentiation, since self-identity comes through an understanding of being different from others."[3]

	Developmental Stage	Chooses to Wear/Would Like to Wear
I. (18–24)	Politics of appearance based predominantly on "fitting in"; dependent on and comfortable with "basics" but peer-related trend items increase in importance.	"Basics": jeans, khakis, T-shirts, iconic sportswear and sneakers (Adidas, Puma, Nike).[1]
II. (24–34+)	Becomes more aware of adult and/or "professional" wardrobes. Begins to seek more fashionable image in order to "move up" and appear more successful.	Tailored clothing; quality, low-end designer pieces; accessories like sunglasses and shoes continue to be a focus.
III. (30–44+)	Fully aware of need to "dress to impress"; desires to expand professional and casual wardrobe for personal gain and to demonstrate "success." Might experiment with high-fashion pieces.	Designer suits and sportswear, leather jackets; soft fibers such as cashmere; timeless "classics" combined with a few fashion-forward status pieces.

[1]Sneakers have become an increasingly important factor and their cult-like status indicates that this category is an important "first step" in developing fashion and design awareness. For more on the cult of the sneaker, see *Sneaker Book: Anatomy of an Industry and an Icon* by Tom Vanderbilt.

Figure 7. Men's Style Cycle

The goal of the Men's Style Cycle is to better explain the male retail experience and develop a criterion for target market merchandising. I've supported this concept with a set of portraits of a random sampling of men, taken on various city streets. (See the insert at the end of chapter 6.)

What's important to note is that from early adulthood, men are distinctly aware of the need to "fit in" (Stage I); however, as their lifestyles change—specifically, when they begin working professional jobs—they become more aware of the need to add tailored garments to their wardrobes (Stage II). By the time they are established in their line of work, their appearance is not only a reflection of who they have become, but also a statement of who they hope to become (Stage III). There are nuances, of course. Come Saturday, the man who wore a suit on Friday is back in his jeans and T-shirt: leisure looks continue to be dominated by sportswear.

If one walks through most department store men's departments with this template in mind, one begins to see that there is confusion about the target audience. Merchandise is too old, too young, too "gay," or too "weird."[4] And men seeking guidance are lost in a mass of brands and styles that lack relevance to one other, and also to the lives they lead. Says Bergdorf Goodman's Robert Burke, "The looks have been too contrived and ridiculous.... Too many things out there are either too of-the-moment or not long-lasting."[5] Which is why, if anything sells, it's consistently the tried-and-true basics (Stage I). In a Cotton, Inc., study, 38.2 percent of men said that even if they didn't need more jeans, they'd probably buy two pairs anyway, while 34.3 percent said they would buy several pairs.[6] The demand for jeans has only become more intense as smaller,

Stage I: The Men's Style Cycle

With Photography by Teru Yoshida

T-shirts and jeans continue to be many men's favorite uniform. Classic, functional, and stereotypically "American." Message T-shirts offer the opportunity to demonstrate an individualist spirit and rock'n'roll swagger. Of all product categories, men will buy larger quantities of T-shirts than they will other items.

The look is intentionally casual but the jacket allows him to make a statement. The layering of T-shirt, sweater, and jacket reveals an extra effort that was made to have a somewhat individualistic look. Layering is a relatively new trend in mixing patterns and fabrics.

The slightly oversized polo and loose flannel shirt mean that there is little attention drawn to his body. It's a "working-class hero" look that is classically all-American and masculine. But even looks such as this one are usually carefully thought out.

The shapeless jeans and oversized polo draw little attention to the body and emphasize that he's a relaxed kind of guy (even if he's not). Accessories continue to be important to men and are used to give style to an otherwise untailored look. The traditionally working-class trucker hat has had a long run as a hipster statement piece. Men will sometimes stretch this look well into their thirties, seemingly in denial that their younger days are behind them.

more exclusive denim brands add new energy to a seemingly saturated market. But this demand may also point to the simple fact that jeans are not only a wardrobe staple for men; they are one item of clothing men feel confident in shopping for because they hold little danger of a fashion faux pas.

For the past fifty or more years, jeans have been a well-documented symbol of youthful rebellion and urban cool. Blue jeans notwithstanding, mainstream clothing stores often miss the mark with younger demographics simply because they overlook the tightrope a young man, in particular, must walk as he tries to expresses himself in the modern world. Writes Sophie Woodward:

> *Identity as expressed through clothing emerges through the relationship between the individual and particular social groups, and what is at stake is credibility, belonging, and standing out. . . . As the sociologist Georg Simmel has argued, the tension between the desire to be part of a social group and the 'individual elevation from it' is a core dynamic to being human, and in turn this is central to the propulsion of fashion change.*[7]

Men, in their desire to escape any number of variables (including youth, class, or ethnicity), simultaneously endeavor to stay true to who they are: to be authentically connected with whichever group is meaningful at that moment. The same man who works in a professional office downtown will take on an altogether different identity when he is in the sports bar.

To move men forward in terms of fashion, one must exercise the utmost care not to undermine the personas they have already

Stage II: Men's Style Cycle

With Photography by Teru Yoshida

It was in the 1990s that men discovered how to mix traditional dress shirts with jeans. This continues to be a popular means of communicating that one has entered the professional world but is still rebellious and not uptight.

The shirt is worn fitted in order to reveal a gym-toned physique. The upturned collar demonstrates suaveness and confidence. The sunglasses add a touch of "I'm cooler than you" to the whole look. This is a Stage II man who will quickly move into Stage III, depending on his profession and salary.

For several years now, men in this stage of the Style Cycle have replaced suit jackets with black synthetic fleece outdoor jackets. They find that it is practical and allows them to appear sporty and casual, even in New York's Financial District. Mid-level managers wearing full suits could risk looking like they're trying to be somebody they're not. Regardless, this style means only having to buy dress pants rather than a whole suit.

Soft knits have grown in popularity with men, especially with the increase in fitness memberships. A relatively "safe" ensemble sets the stage for more fashion forward pieces.

created for themselves in the eyes of their peers. So how do you build demand for suits, sport coats, and basics—or for that matter, for trend-driven merchandise? One solution is to offer men classics with a twist. Neil Cusnetz, president at Robert Graham, says, "We need to get a little younger in look and feel and attitude… including fashion colors."[8] In other words, take those basics and update them by using details and color (Stage II). Other industry executives have suggested increasing the availability of "performance-rich" clothing, which gives customers added value. This solution also helps bridge the divide between the mundane and the flamboyant, so that men can subtly achieve a new standard of sameness. Indeed, they "fit in," but with a discreet level of stylishness that elevates them from the rest.

Fiber content is actually a key component of what a man looks for when he shops, and natural fabrics (cotton and wool) play an important role. In fact, according to another Cotton, Inc., study, 52.5 percent of men check fabric content when purchasing a garment; when it comes to deciding what to buy, fiber content comes second only to price (76.7 percent check the price).[9] In another study, it was shown that 59 percent of men between the ages of twenty-five and fifty-five (compared with 41 percent of women), make quality-driven apparel purchases.[x]

A return to dressing well and dressing up is a trend that is increasingly resonating with men for a variety of reasons. The man who ends up wholly embracing fashion and style and splurges on designer clothes and watches (Stage III) does so because the results have proven themselves. As one interview subject told me (half-jokingly), "We dress well because we want to get laid."[12] Will Manzer, president of Perry Ellis menswear, says that "the whole concept of dressing better and the idea of

Stage III: Men's Style Cycle

With Photography by Teru Yoshida

This is a man who is confident in tailored clothing and is now well-versed in the effect of a suit on his persona. He has carefully accessorized the gray flannel with a purple tie and matching handkerchief. The messenger bag ensures that the look doesn't become too fussy or uptight.

While the jacket is too oversized for his frame, he has combined it with jeans and an unbuttoned shirt to show that he is stylish enough to not have to wear a tie.

The retro yachting club look is conspicuously "to the manor born" and could easily be influenced by Ralph Lauren's upper-class Americana style. The overall look, while slightly cliché, shows that he is confident enough to dress up rather than down.

The black tailored pants, black sweater with pushed up sleeves, and messenger bag show confidence and self-awareness. Men in Stage III are usually cognizant that a defined silhouette is the most important step in having "style."

Wilkes Bashford:
Style Scion of the West Coast

There are few boutique retailers who can claim an over sixty year history of success, let alone ones in which the founder is still around to enjoy that success. That mantle can go to Wilkes Bashford, who, since 1966, has been the go-to man for the best in tailored menswear. Bashford wears his style on his well-tailored sleeve. It was he who introduced the biggest names in better menswear to the wild and woolly West Coast city of San Francisco—names like Ralph Lauren, Armani, and Versace. Today, Bashford's four Northern California stores (San Francisco, Stanford Shopping Center, Carmel Plaza, and St. Helena) continue to operate with great success, and as a result, a whole new generation of men are discovering the understated beauty of a Brioni.

The '60s in San Francisco was a heady time. The love beads, T-shirts, and Levi's jeans were hardly the kind of thing Bashford, who then was only in his thirties, was interested in selling. But social and political changes of the time ushered in a new perspective on how men dressed. "By the late '60s, there were flower children everywhere and that rebellious spirit [had broken] down a lot of barriers for how young men could dress," remembers Bashford. "Men were suddenly asking: why can't I wear a brightly colored shirt or grow my hair long? Why not tailor my suit like Mick [Jagger's] and wear it with boots?"[11]

Elsewhere in the world, European designers were influencing the Americans with a new kind of tailoring, and Bashford was taking note. "This is when we started to see the men's designer—people who gave menswear the same respect as women's wear. People like Pierre Cardin. He radically changed the meaning of the suit and gave it a style most people had never seen before."

Bashford opened his first boutique in San Francisco on August 11, 1966, and within a short time, his store became known as the place where the city's stylish men—men like former San Francisco mayor Willie Brown, his most famous client—went to see what was new. Bashford's slogan at the time, "Menswear for the bold conservative," still holds true in many ways.

"Back then, our competition was Brooks Brothers and Joseph Kirk. Not that there was anything wrong with what they offered, but when I gave men Armanis to try on, they suddenly saw themselves differently. And that's what a men's store should do: show men how to look their best—not just how to look like everybody else."

With seven floors of retail, the San Francisco store now includes women's wear, sportswear, and home décor. Style doesn't come cheap: we're talking $5,000 suits, $2,000 briefcases, and $1,500 handmade boots. But make no mistake, Bashford is a man with a plan, and that plan has been to serve a clearly identified customer—something many men's retailers lose track of. "To be a successful men's store you must have a vision of who you want to appeal to," says Bashford. "If you establish your vision and direct your efforts towards that, then you can build a meaningful customer relationship. The mistake most people make is that they're not consistent."

In any one of his four stores, you won't find flash-in-the-pan merchandise. This is still fashion for the "bold conservative" but without the flights of fancy. Bashford's consistency is in making sure his merchandise foundation is rock-solid, which allows him to experiment in other areas. But he does that cautiously. "We carried Thom Browne. I don't think our customer really understands that kind of suit, though. His jackets are about two inches shorter, so half his seat is showing. I'm not sure if that's a look many men will appreciate."

Bashford has shown a knack for weathering the storm, whether economic or fashion. But even with a crashing Wall Street, he says men know that, now more than ever, how they look speaks to their ability and stability. "A sophisticated man knows that how they dress determines how they will be perceived. There's an intrinsic value that comes of that." Fashion everywhere took a hit in the 1990s when grunge—that slouchy, sloppy, rag-tag look—took hold. Couple that with casual Friday and you've got every retailer's worst nightmare. But Bashford made it through both, thanks to some savvy strategy: offer casual, but make it casual quality. (Think cashmere sweaters, relaxed wool pants, and a sensibility that would make any man feel like Cary Grant in *To Catch a Thief*.)

So how does Wilkes Bashford stay relevant in an increasingly competitive retail market? The legendary haberdasher says the rules are simple and set in stone:

"First of all, make sure they get a clear picture of your major brand names that set the tone and standard for what you sell. For Wilkes Bashford, it's Brioni and Kiton. This gets them to understand the kind of style you believe in as a store."

Next, guide them in the elements of style:

"Show sportswear and shoes, and let them know this is a place where they can discover an image of who they are by mixing things together."

And most importantly, develop a family of sales associates who meet the diverse range of clients out there:

"Ideally, you have a diverse set of staff who satisfy and can communicate with different demographics and personalities. They need to be able to confidently communicate and guide the customer, and really listen and hear what their needs are. They also need to be sophisticated. It's ultimately their responsibility to help move the client forward and evolve his personal style."

good taste is coming back into vogue—fashion that makes a man look better and feel better.... Men want to be proud of themselves and proud of what they're wearing. Everybody's upgrading and looking for brands with equity, looking for a great price-value, and looking for newness."[13]

And that's very telling. The problem is that so many stores still don't know how to speak to the male customer, nor do they know how to grow him into a profitable target market. While women are provided with a host of media messages about trends, men are given significantly less information about style. What is communicated in advertising or even in mainstream men's magazines can sometimes smack too much of "big city" style that doesn't always resonate with the regular guy. Again, this is an area that is changing as we speak.

Retail analysts believe that tailored classics are the real winners in menswear. A suit has the longevity and wearability that can take a man from out-of-work to back-to-work. But men are not buying just any suit. According to many retailers, what's selling are suits with details: hand-stitching, colorful linings, and quality materials. In the words of Tom Kalenderian, executive vice president for menswear at Barneys, "It's not about revolution, it's about evolution."[14] In other words, it's about an evolved product that aligns itself with the evolved man (or the one who wants to become that way). These are men who are looking for clothes that won't draw unwanted attention but will give a clear indication that they have taste.

Take for example, Brooks Brothers' recent turnaround act. It included hiring Thom Browne to design its higher profile, luxury line of men's essentials, dubbed the "Black Fleece Collection." It's a bold move coming from a brand that for years had completely lost its mojo and needed a major shot in the arm. It worked. In 2007, Black Fleece added another $10 million to Brooks's $800 million in annual sales; by the end of 2008, Brooks had opened its first free-standing Black Fleece

An advertisement for Brooks Brothers' Black Fleece collection designed by Thom Browne. After nearly two decades of stagnancy, the brand is poised to re-enter the modern era of men's clothiers.

boutique in SoHo. The man in the gray flannel suit is now the man in black fleece.

So what's the formula for a great menswear assortment? It starts with the store itself and its point of view. A great store, one with credibility, needs to be able to present the basics and do it well. If the suit is the foundation of a man's wardrobe, then stores need to sell tailored menswear that has a distinct point of view—not 500 competing points of view. Marshal Cohen, senior retail analyst for the NPD Group, summarizes it this way: "Men don't need to see forty different pairs of black pants, the way women like to see…. They want to see three pairs of black pants, have some clerk tell him what to wear with them, and move on."[15] Retailers need to find a new balance between safety and risk in their buys. Says designer Joseph Abboud, "Playing it safe isn't safe anymore… you have to take some kind of estimated risk to gain a more intelligent presentation and more exclusive product so that people will come to your store."[16]

Rebranding the Man

The most successful stores are those that consistently appraise their brand concept. From the mega-store to the corner boutique, change—while staying true to your vision—is what keeps a brand fresh and vital to the customer.

Menswear is unique in that men generally don't respond well to radical change. Like their favorite bars or barbershops, the hallmarks and heritage of clothing are important; they signify integrity and dependability.

Fatal errors can be as simple as spending thousands on a new logo and believing that it will change the perception of the brand. To rebrand successfully, one must revisit square one and ask: What's my contribution to the marketplace? Who is my customer?

A great men's store evolves alongside its customer, but always one step ahead so that it is the facilitator of change.

Here are some things that should be part of a normal review of a menswear business strategy.

1) **Renew, Refresh, and Revise.** The market is constantly changing and so are men. The assumptions you made when you first started your business may not hold true today. Think about other areas you can capitalize on. Offer new services and explore new product categories, such as a bolder accessories offer.

2) **Make a plan and stick to it.** Once you've determined where you want your brand to go, write a creative brief that offers clear direction for your stakeholders. That means key objectives, research and analysis, target market studies, budgets, and revised staffing roles. All of this information needs to be packaged specifically for the people involved (i.e., the sales staff need to briefed.)

3) **Build on your brand equity.** Just because you want to expand your brand and target a new audience doesn't mean you should alienate your existing customer. Be strategic in how you switch gears, and try to regulate the amount of atrophy that may come from too sudden a change.

4) **God is in the details.** A series of small changes to your brand experience can often have as much of an effect as a total makeover. Go for the low-hanging fruit and explore the changes you can make to your packaging or the addition of free delivery. Explore how strategic partnerships and co-marketing can reinforce your brand positioning.

5) **Act like a customer.** Go through each of the touchpoints of the customer experience, from calling the store to using the Web site. Have family or friends give you constructive criticism on the store experience.

6) **Review the competition.** Keep careful notes of what the competition is doing and use this to leverage your rebranding process.

7) **Keep the end goal in mind.** Very often, people get caught up in adding flash and dash and forget about the substance. New technology should be less about show and more about optimizing the level of customer service you can offer.

Men shop as much for what they hope to become as for what they need. With this in mind, a store's assortment is as much about a quality selection as it is about giving a man the opportunity to look into the future.

Men are aspiring to dress differently, and that's only going to increase as sports and film celebrities continue to make dressing well an expression of masculine self-assurance. "It's going to require some really high-profile people—politicians, opinion leaders—to make a difference in how men dress, but it's definitely happening," says Saks Fifth Avenue's David Pilnick. "Look what happened when Nicholas Sarkozy wore Dior Homme. Suddenly a president is a fashion plate. If men see someone like that getting kind of edgy, that definitely helps a store justify a brand."[17] U.S. President Barack Obama, not to mention his wife Michelle, has already caused a ripple effect on American fashion, with fashion journalists breathlessly invoking the Obama White House as the next "Camelot" (in reference to the Kennedy Administration). Alas, Obama's predecessor, George W. Bush, and his wife, Laura, had little to no impact in positioning American style.

Chapter 6: The Take-Away

To create the optimal menswear environment is to create an authenticity of both store experience and branded product. An authentic message fosters loyalty to the store by virtue of the fact that all of the isolated components of the experience lock together into a seamless whole. The most successful stores are those that have been strategic in creating dynamic and distinctive in-store experiences that make the linear experience of product and purchase personalized and seemingly unique.

This chapter's Men's Style Cycle shows how men's fashion needs and desires are a progression in three stages. As men mature from adolescence to adulthood, they discover a growing desire to simultaneously fit in and distinguish themselves from the masses. Success, and the demonstration of that success, becomes a means of self-expression through a carefully constructed self-image. Research indicates that men shop for garments that are inherently performance-rich or functional in nature. But given the opportunity, men will make informed decisions, provided there is a means of obtaining that information. A great store has the basics to satisfy a man's needs, but also offers a distinct point of view. Men shop as much for who they hope to become as they do for what they need. The ideal store is like friend and mentor, offering the right balance of affirmation and evolutionary advice. It gives a man the opportunity to look into the future of who he might become.

CHAPTER SEVEN

Retailers Making Their Mark: Who Leads? Who Follows?

B y now, every retailer knows that selling to men is no easy task. But that knowledge doesn't always translate into savvy choices and strategic action. Over the past ten years it's been the boutique retailers who have made the greatest strides towards transforming the kind of merchandise offered to men. Large specialty retailers like Barneys or Jeffrey in New York are unburdened by the expectations consumers have of department stores—namely, that they should offer everything, and at the most competitive pricing. But whether large or small, department store or boutique, men's retailers face challenges equal to their advantages. They simply differ in each case.

If we break down the most critical criterion for the average consumer (let alone the average *male* consumer) we can see that both the boutique retailer and department store retailer face unique challenges (*Figure 7*).

But it is boutique retailers who are the most favorably positioned to satisfy their target customer, simply by virtue of their clarity of message and ability to offer a highly focused and branded experience. By and large, men respond to boutique store environments because they are easily understood

Success or Challenge Factor	Boutique Retailer	Department Store Retailer
Assortment	Sometimes limited, with an emphasis on certain product categories (premium denim, for instance).	Large assortment satisfying multiple customer profiles—but sometimes bewildering in the multiplicity of choices.
Style/Point of View	Unique brands, progressive style—but if it's not "you," you're out.	Often mainstream brands and styles; difficult to discern a store's point of view.
Customer Service	More personalized, easier to get service and advice; stronger product knowledge.	Erratic customer service and spotty product knowledge.
Navigation	Easy to enter and navigate. Smaller square footage makes emphasis less on "shop and go" and more on "stay and explore."	Complicated entry and navigation—often requiring passing through cosmetics and other departments; too much indiscriminate choice of product spread across too much space. Emphasis is usually placed on boldly placed signage logos to attract shoppers to branded areas—but they diminish hierarchy and cloud store's point-of-view. "Shop and go" atmosphere resembles supermarket.
Price/Value	Higher price point, few sale periods.	Competitive pricing, more frequent sale periods.

Figure 8. Retailer Category: Successes and Challenges

Location	Can be inconvenient; decision to go there often contingent on attractive adjacencies (shops, restaurants, etc.) and convenient parking.	Usually in central location. Adjacencies allow for price/style comparison. Usually convenient (and free) parking.
Atmosphere	Can feel too exclusive and intimidating; service can be overbearing for male customer (too much attention).	Department store atmosphere is familiar, it's easy to pass through unnoticed. Easy to self-serve. Busy atmosphere can allow one to shop undisturbed.
Fitting Rooms	One-on-one service makes trying on clothes easier, with efficient exchange of sizes and "looks," rapid stock checks, and helpful suggestions.	Fitting rooms are often isolated; and customer service can mean waiting for salesperson to bring other sizes, stock checks, etc.

Figure 8. Continued

compared to the confusing messaging that comes from department stores. Where department stores once ruled men's retailing, boutique retailers are now capitalizing on their opportunity to offer a focused assortment, an authentic point of view, customized service, and a distinctive atmosphere. However, each environment has its fair share of challenges. While boutique retailers score well with savvy sophisticates, the Regular Joe will generally visit a department store rather than a specialty store. Where boutiques triumph, however, is in customer service. Says San Francisco's Wilkes Bashford: "The thing about boutiques is that they have the flexibility to move fast and know the customer much better. Department stores have the advantage of better resources in finance and research, and they also reach a wider audience thanks to their substantial marketing and advertising budgets. This gives them a lot more clout with the customer simply because they're much more visible."[1]

Like many department stores, Saks Fifth Avenue is always trying to develop stronger strategies for making its men's department an obvious choice for clothes. Says David Pilnick, senior vice president of international business ventures for Saks: "Making a store matter means making sure that the customer feels as though he is understood there and [that] there's at least some product that speaks to him."[2] Research by WSL Strategic Retail showed that by 2006, 74 percent of men were making independent decisions on what to buy for themselves. But even now, they're still shying away from premium retailers, instead heading to the discounters. No wonder Men's Wearhouse isn't feeling much pain these days, considering that its price points are 20 to 30 percent below those at department stores—not to mention the fact that it has smaller store environments that essentially focus on one thing: business attire.

Meanwhile, as the youth market becomes more and more knowledgeable and willing to adopt new fashion, the main-stream market steadily interprets it for the masses. Consider the considerable influence of the urban, underground retailer, from the youth-oriented, limited-edition sneaker store to the small, local boutique selling merchandise from young, fresh designers. Their impact is well documented by trend analysts and can be seen everywhere, from department stores to the couture houses of Paris. The sneaker store alone has become a trend-setting benchmark for design and cultural trends in fashion and music and has allowed brands like Nike and Puma to experiment with new merchandise and increase their "cool" factor. The young trendsetter seeks out these smaller stores where individuality rules and premium (meaning no one else has it) merchandise can be found.

It's So You:
Customization Gets Personal

One of the fastest growing trends in retail is customization. In the battle for the customer dollar, there is nothing that makes a customer feel a little more special than having something made to their specifications. It's akin to having a restaurant chef prepare your off-the-menu dish request. Luxury brands like Gucci jumped on the trend during the dot-com boom with made-to-order handbags, custom shoes, and made-to-measure suits. Others have experimented with selling a limited number of collection pieces in certain stores (usually only in flagships).

Customization is a service that can become an important brand signature of a store—even if some customers don't opt to use it. Take Land's End, which offers a pair of custom-made jeans for $80. Custom merchandise typically runs 20–30 percent more than off the rack items, but in a Jupiter Research study, more than half of consumers were willing to pay $10 more to order a custom pair of $50 pants.[3] While the number of men who opt for custom-made suits is still relatively low, there are many who choose made-to-measure suits, which can often have the look and feel of custom-made.

Designer Thom Browne, who creates the Black Fleece collection for Brooks Brothers and sells his eponymous line in Bergdorf Goodman, says, "I wanted to bring that custom sensibility to the

A better fit is only part of our promise.

Strict quality standards ensure your Lands' End Custom™ garment not only fits you properly, but also exceeds your expectations on workmanship and durability. 'Cause what's the use of having a great fitting garment if it doesn't last?

Lands' End Custom clothing is Guaranteed. Period.®

younger man in a way that isn't that fussy custom-clothing experience... my customer is more into the sensibility of the whole thing."[4] On a different level, consider the boon for Banana Republic when it was one of the first mass merchants to offer free alterations. For menswear, there are numerous instances where customization can help shape the image of a brand—and of the man who shops there. Men are increasingly willing to pay more for custom tailoring in suits, shirts, and shoes. Another thing that makes customization a home-run for a brand is when it's free.

Two key trends stand out, trends that continue to deeply influence the specialty retail business across the board:

1) **Specialization:** A store must establish a distinct point of view by means of its product, service, and partnerships (music, lifestyle products, etc.), and it must resonate with the customer as authentic and on-trend. The store must be perceived as reliably ahead of the curve;

2) **Exclusives and Limited Editions:** The particular store may be the only location where one can obtain certain exclusive and limited edition merchandise, either designed and developed by the store brand or by a designer to be sold exclusively at that store. This makes it a destination as well as a recognized authority on the latest and greatest. If one is associated with the store and the product, one is automatically cool. If the product is created by a designer (such as what Isaac Mizrahi did for Target), the store has officially been "blessed" by the designer, and the store leverages that designer's cool factor.

Across the U.S., there are retailers both large and small who are taking risks and exploring ways of growing their male customer base. However, they are proceeding slowly and cautiously: men, unlike women, seldom give a store a second chance.

What follows are examples of stores that I believe have challenged traditional men's retail and have managed to position themselves with their respective target customerd as both mentor and arbiter of cool.

Lombardi Sports, San Francisco: Training Men in Fitness—and Fashion

Lombardi Sports is a sixty-year-old sporting goods store in San Francisco that had been doing just fine selling camping gear, tennis rackets, athletic shoes, and bikes. It was and is consistently one of the city's top destinations for serious sports enthusiasts. As a stand-alone store—there is only one—it has never bothered to pay much attention to the larger chain stores. Why? Because the family-owned operation has put a premium on customer service—they know many of their shoppers on a first-name basis. Says Ken Lombardi, marketing director, "We've gotten to a point now where our customers already know they can depend on us to be right about athletic gear. Now we're getting their confidence about fashion and leisure gear."[5] The company

Lombardi Sports in San Francisco. The sixty-year-old store has evolved from a strictly outdoor sporting supplier to a lifestyle store with designer casualwear. The concept resonates with customers all over the Bay Area.

has always been at the forefront; in 1977, they were Nike's first San Francisco dealer for the Waffle training shoe.

It was in the early 1990s that Lombardi says he began to see a significant shift in their customer's lifestyle. He saw an opportunity to satisfy an almost subconscious need: looking good *after* working out or playing sports. Lombardi Sports began exploring what had been, until then, uncharted territory for a sporting goods store. It started selling fashion. Today, about half of the selling floor is devoted to strictly fashion lifestyle merchandise. Maz Hattori is Lombardi's buying manager. "We started experimenting with surf wear, and then I took some risks and brought in some stuff that kind of bridged surf with fashion... brands like Ben Sherman, Blue Marlin, and Von Dutch."[6] Von Dutch, the brand that in the late 1990s brought white trash chic to young Hollywood, is one example of a brand Lombardi carried before anyone else in the region. Now Von Dutch is not selling as steadily and Hattori has replaced it with additional premium denim—a strong seller for the store. Another strategy? Tap into the growing men's grooming market. The store now carries Kiehl's products. "A lot of guys are still kind of awkward about going into a Kiehl's store to buy moisturizer. But here, we have it right by the check-out, so it's an easy impulse buy," says Hattori. When a brand or style doesn't work, the Lombardi team uses what they learned to inform future buys. Says Ken Lombardi, "I tell our buyers, if you're going to fail, fail forward."

The store is not glamorous, nor does it aspire to be. Aisles are filled to the brim with racks and shelves full of clothes, and brand logos and signs compete for wall space. Hattori says their customer likes it this way because it makes navigation easy (in a sports store, customers typically shop by brand). The other important tool they use to communicate with the male customer? Mannequins. "If a guy can't see something in context with other clothes like jeans or accessories, then he might not understand it," says Hattori. It's a strategy that's paying off, with profit from fashion merchandise at roughly 20 to 30 percent of total revenue and an annual increase of almost 10 percent a year. "Our vendors definitely have more confidence with how we've developed our store," says Lombardi. Customers are confident, too. "They trust us. They know that if we carry it, it's because we believe in it."

Oslo's, Seattle: The Neighborhood Men's Store

Oslo's is a 1,000-square-foot store located in Seattle's lush Queen Anne neighborhood. While many still don't think of fashion when they think of the Pacific Northwest, Seattle has

Oslo's in Seattle. Owner John MacDowell saw a need for quality menswear outside of a shopping mall, with the added benefit of an old-fashioned barber.

exploded with trendy lifestyle offerings, from cutting-edge restaurants to distinctive fashion boutiques. But in 2005, Oslo's
owner John MacDowell saw a need that wasn't fulfilled by
Nordstrom, Macy's, or Banana Republic. His choice to open a
neighborhood store makes sense because MacDowell believes
that men are generally averse to high-traffic, high-impact shopping malls and districts. A neighborhood store has the opportunity to offer a discreet, low-key, and personalized ambiance in
a setting that is distinctly casual and suburban. Like the corner
coffee shop, it's not trying to be anything more than what it
is—an important factor in targeting male customers.

MacDowell says that, even in Seattle, men are changing,
and while they're not dressing like guys in Los Angeles or San
Francisco, they're certainly aware that fashion enhances one's
profile. "I began to sense that guys were taking steps toward
wanting to show off their efforts at the gym, look a bit classier
as they got out of their sports cars, and show off their new
Microsoft wealth [Microsoft's headquarters is in Redmond,
just outside Seattle]."[7] More importantly, MacDowell feels that
men want an environment that mentors them in how to build
a functional and stylish wardrobe. "They love it when we pull
five pairs of jeans and explain the fits. They enjoy being made
over," MacDowell says, adding, "it's best if we have a woman
salesperson who can tell them their ass looks hot in that pair
of jeans."[7]

A big plus for Oslo's atmosphere is its lack of pretension.
MacDowell's dog—Oslo, who lent his name to the store—is
the mascot and unofficial greeter to all who enter. But it's the
store's barbershop that lends cachet and a sense of homespun
comfort and old-fashioned authenticity. "The barbershop

literally and figuratively has a buzz going on," says MacDowell. "Differentiating the barber with certification from The Art of Shaving™ made a huge difference in the press coverage we got. If we had the space, we'd actually do more."[7] MacDowell admits he's still working out the kinks in his merchandise assortment, but says he's confident that the future for Oslo's—and menswear—is bright. "Retailing isn't like healthcare. We're not curing cancer, but if I can help a guy feel a bit more confident walking into an interview or going to a party, or look stylish on parent-teacher night, then I've hit my goal."[7]

John Varvatos: Swaggering Classics

In less than ten years, John Varvatos has grown his brand into eight free-standing retail stores with an estimated $80 million in annual sales. His menswear collections are built on the foundations of old-world tailoring and timeless classics, but with a modern, American rock'n'roll edge. The brand is now a full-fledged lifestyle brand, with belts, bags, footwear, eyewear, skincare, fragrance, and, of course, clothes.

His stores are typically raw, industrial spaces decorated with a pastiche of flea market finds: old rolling racks for clothes, leather club chairs, and antique fireplaces. Whether it's a beautifully tailored black wool coat, or a worn leather biker jacket, Varvatos has managed to capture the right formula of masculine cool without being too fussy and overwrought. Varvatos says he always stays true to his beliefs about menswear. "I think there are a lot of guys who want what my vision is all about," says Varvatos. "I think it's more about guys wanting to step out a little bit—to push the envelope. I don't think you should wear anything that you're uncomfortable in. I call it an evolution,

The John Varvatos store on New York's Bowery is located in the former home of the landmark live music venue, CBGB. This location lends the brand a sense of rock'n'roll authenticity.

not a revolution."[8] From beautifully tailored suits and shirts to hand-knit sweaters and enormous scarves, Varvatos indeed pushes the envelope—without ever making a man step too far into discomfort. His stores stock all manner of menswear essentials, but he is known to add vintage denim, rock T-shirts, accessories, and books. Sometimes he'll even pop in some rare vinyl records from his personal collection. Varvatos' approach could be compared to Paul Smith's, but the brand conveys a moody romance that draws considerable influence from the rock music that's inspired him since his Detroit childhood.

In 2008, he opened three boutiques within months of each other in New York (in addition to a store already located on Mercer Street), San Francisco, and Malibu. The New York store is in the former home of the legendary CBGB club on Bowery, a location that couldn't be more in tune with the brand. Varvatos chose to change the space as little as possible, and the walls still have the graffiti and concert stickers from the venue's halcyon days. It's the kind of environment which serves to highlight the brand's message, one that would make any man want to drop some cash to feel like a rock star. Just in case he's inspired, a small stage, ready for impromptu concerts, is set with classic instruments and amps from the 1970s.

"The Liquor Store" by J.Crew: A Chain Brand Goes Grassroots

Compared to other major chains, J.Crew is relatively small—it only has 267 stores—but 2007 revenues were a not-too-shabby $1.3 billion. CEO Mickey Drexler is no stranger to experimenting with retail (consider his rise and rise—and fall—with Old Navy and Gap), so it's easy to see why he's ready to gamble again, this time with an exclusive focus on menswear. He has worked hard to turn the J.Crew brand around, and even in unsteady economic times, he has tinkered with styles and prices. Today, J.Crew is the darling of mainstream boutique retailing, and Drexler is prepared to bank on men's clothing as an exciting new frontier for the brand.

But can the brand get men to embrace its decidedly preppy sensibility with an expanded (and even more expensive) menswear collection and a dedicated men's store? Time will tell. The brand is testing the waters with a unique concept store in Manhattan's TriBeCa that has an off-the-radar approach: take an old liquor store in a historic building and make it a men's store. There is no sign (it still says "liquor store," and that has become its name), and the inside still has many of the original fittings and fixtures. It's an almost-pop-up store approach that radiates authenticity—especially for a brand like J.Crew.

The J.Crew Men's Store in New York City is located in a former liquor store and bar. J.Crew has used the store to experiment with new product lines and an editorial point of view, offering vintage pieces and a hip, urban feel.

So what's in store? J.Crew's senior VP of merchandising Todd Snyder has stocked the shop with the "best of the best," from limited-edition J.Crew pieces to vintage accessories like refurbished Rolex watches and classic vinyl records. It's an edited assortment that not only has a point of view but speaks to how Snyder believes modern men want to shop. "There is no one place to shop. You have to go to at least six stores to get everything you need to have the best wardrobe."[9] Conversely, Snyder's aim is to offer the best, all in one place. It's a bold—and some might even say risky—strategy for a mainstream fashion brand to think it could be such a store. But Snyder says that this concept allows the brand to experiment and innovate by combining a boutique atmosphere with the lifestyle experience. "There is a a great opportunity for J.Crew to pick up the Abercrombie & Fitch graduates. The children of the baby boomers are three years away from getting into their twenties, and there are not a lot of retailers that are well positioned for this phenomenon right now,"[10] says Brian Tunick, analyst at J.P. Morgan Chase. That couldn't be more true, and while Gap continues to fumble, the competition is narrowing in. Along with J.Crew, Abercrombie and American Eagle are both looking to extend their reach.

Snyder says that the Liquor Store concept is where he and his team can further develop the J.Crew men's brand as the arbiter of cool in a setting that couldn't be cooler. The unfussy, downtown chic of an old liquor store naturally lends itself to that. In this environment, store staff can guide men in their sartorial pursuits. "A man needs to know the two or three perfect pairs of shoes to own, the best jeans wash, the best chino fit, the best jacket, the perfect suit, and the correct width of tie," says Snyder. He continues, "It all starts with the shoes and accessories. They're the foundation of a men's wardrobe." Surprised he'd start here? In 2007, J.Crew tried selling classic Red Wing shoes and sold 2,000 units. They were the best selling shoe in the company's history and even outsold women's shoes. While it could be said that J.Crew's concept might only work in major metropolitan cities where men are generally more sophisticated, the brand's bold experiment has all the earmarks of a great men's store concept that could easily trickle down to cities across the country.

Chapter 7: The Take-Away

Boutique retailers and department stores each face their own challenges in successfully serving the male customer. Boutiques are the most favorably positioned by virtue of the facts that they are more tightly focused in their assortment and that the service is more personalized. Boutiques are also able to move on trends more quickly than department stores. But department stores are still where men typically go, perhaps out of habit and because large-scale retailers generate awareness through sizable marketing budgets. Lombardi Sports, a small, local sporting goods store in San Francisco, is one example of how a merchant has expanded its expertise to include more lifestyle-driven merchandise without compromising its integrity as a classic sporting goods purveyor. Oslo's, a specialty men's boutique in Seattle, challenges the more mainstream selection and style of big box retailers with a sharply focused brand selection and a barbershop that gives the store an added edge over other stores, plus a fun, old-fashioned ambiance. John Varvatos has created retail environments that feel edgy and cool, and his Bowery store in the old CBGB bar is a perfect expression of the brand's image and spirit. Varvatos banked on the space's provenance and allowed it to enhance his own brand with a distinctly rock'n'roll atmosphere. J.Crew's men's concept store in New York is a bold experiment in how a chain retailer can get its groove back with a boutique feel that could certainly feel right with men and boost the brand's position as a men's destination.

CHAPTER EIGHT

Getting the Goods: Let the Merchandise Tell the Story

Beginning in 2004, "premium sportswear" came to define the renaissance of menswear. Bona fide classics like Lacoste and Levi's took center stage, as did new brands that gave men a more tailored, fresh appearance without sacrificing comfort. Industry periodical *DNR* called it "The New, New Thing." Stores discovered that there was in fact some substance behind the "metrosexual" hype and that men were ready to wear new and innovative fashions by designers they'd probably never heard of. While men generally shop out of necessity and are more likely to pay full price than women, they'll still look for a bargain. Three out of every four men's sportswear items sold in department stores are purchased on sale, with dress shirts and casual pants being the most frequently bought at discount, and jeans the least. On average, shoppers paid $14 below the ticket price. Consumers have been trained to wait for sale season (and with some department stores, when *isn't* there a sale?), making it increasingly difficult for retailers to build profit margins, especially in menswear. But can that change?

Let's pose the question differently: Will the industry make change worthwhile? Mainstream department stores have often stumbled in their attempt to embrace men's fashion evolution. While they've invested heavily in new brands and smaller labels, they continue to merchandise the "new" as though it were somehow a separate department from the "old" (the suits, shirts, ties, and polos that are the staple of a men's department). Endeavoring to build some momentum, Saks Fifth Avenue has gone big with the idea of "premium"—more fashion-forward merchandise with an even stronger point of view—in roughly sixty-three stores. Says one former Saks merchandiser, "The category has become very credible; it's one of the hopes of the men's business."[1] Bloomingdale's and Bergdorf Goodman are also jumping on the premium bandwagon; ultimately, however, these are retailers that speak more to the moneyed fashion elite than to the middlebrow customer.

In order for the male customer to understand the merchandise, it needs to be framed in a way that that makes sense and can be instantly read as "masculine." The department store suffers in this regard, because menswear—unlike women's wear—needs a stronger context and point of view to make that happen. Department stores are often hindered by brand agreements that force them to emphasize the vendor rather than offer a unique, customized message that speaks to the individual consumer. On the other hand, a boutique has a greater opportunity for authenticity and clarity of message simply by virtue of its independence, smaller size, and concentrated point of view. Durand Guion, fashion director for Macy's West, admits that keeping up with the evolving male customer is not always easy for a department store. "He has become faster and smarter and will not accept fashion just because it is sitting on the sales floor. Determining the proper flow of merchandise

The 'Green' Man:
Does Eco-Fashion Really Matter?

Once upon a time, ecologically correct clothing was hopelessly linked to hippies and vegans and no retailer saw any need to carry such clothes. Eco-clothing meant strange looking, homemade garb that looked like organic bread. In the 1990s, there was a passing popularity of messenger bags made of used tires or automobile seat covers. "Green" fashion was a novelty rather than a necessity in the minds of most consumers.

But with an increase in concern over the state of the environment, many are embracing the idea of responsible consumption. Meanwhile, designers and manufacturers are innovating new ways of working with organic and sustainable materials. Even luxury brands like Stella McCartney are finding ways to make a political statement look chic. Elsewhere, brands like Bamford and Sons, Rogan Gregory (who launched Loomstate with Scott Hahn), and John Patrick Organic are bringing eco-chic to major retailers like Barneys New York. But does organic or sustainably produced clothing really resonate with a male customer? There is no simple answer. Men do buy such items, but their reason isn't always because of how it was produced.

In a 2001 survey, 6 percent of respondents said they are interested in buying apparel, footwear, and accessories that are "ecologically friendly." By 2006, that number rose to 18 percent.[2] And global sales of organic cotton goods rose from $245 million in 2001 to $1.07 billion in 2006, according to Organic Exchange, an environmental advocacy group. That number has only increased—even with a slowed economy.

Now, more and more major brands are getting on the green bandwagon. Levi

Strauss and Co. has developed eco jeans made of organic cotton, as has Mavi jeans. The prices are considerably higher than each brand's basic lines: Levi's Eco jeans retail for about $70—that's roughly $25 more than a regular pair of 501s. Nike, one of the world's major consumers of organic cotton, is taking a long-term strategic approach: the company plans to use at least five percent organic cotton in all of its cotton products by 2010. But there is actually not enough supply of organic cotton to meet the demand: less than 1 percent of the world's cotton is actually organic. And unlike home appliances, which are regulated and required to show compliance with certain standards of energy conservation, there are no actual rules for clothing manufacturers. For shoppers, there continues to be a lot of confusion over what "sustainable," "organic," or even "recycled" actually mean. "Just because something is made from an organic fiber doesn't mean it's great for the environment," says Jeff Shafer, founder of Agave Denimsmith. "You have to think about the entire process, from dyes to washing to packaging to printing. It's not that easy to do."[3]

Meanwhile consumer demand for eco-fashion remains fairly small and isn't estimated to grow, according to Andrew Winston, founder of Winston Eco-Strategies and co author of *Green to Gold*. What generally makes more of an impact is *where* a garment was manufactured, and the ethical standards that impacted its manufacture, such as whether child labor was involved. U.K. retailer Marks & Spencer, for instance, has made considerable inroads in supporting farmers in developing countries and using only certified fair trade cotton (a fair trade product is one that is produced by well-paid workers and under regulations of social and environmental standards).[4] In the end, though, men still shop for comfort, price, and quality, and getting them to pay more for what appears to be the same product as the less expensive version is still a challenge. Less impact on the environment is certainly a plus, but it's not a determining factor for making a purchase—at least not yet. "It's taken food companies fifteen years to get to the point where people are willing to pay for organic," says Ty Bowers, co founder of premium men's label Vessel, "so it will take some time for people to understand the organic fashion thing." Just as important, when a company has integrated environmental responsibility into its core values, there is a deeper potential to demonstrate to the customer the integrity of the product and of the brand itself.

and having the right size, color, and style in store—when he wants it—is key."[5] Writes one retail analyst, "Retailers cannot look at a trend and decide to change their stores overnight. The most successful stores are the ones that are consumer-driven and prepared to adjust their focus season-to-season by listening to their customers."

Thus, the challenge lies in creating men's departments that have a clear "story." While women tend to shop with a distinct agenda (and buy by brand and even by outfit), men typically shop by category, seeking to satisfy a specific need. For example, middle-of-the-road retailers like Men's Wearhouse and Jos. A. Bank attract men looking for "performance" fabrics (stain-resistant pants or wrinkle-free shirts). And research from NPD Group certainly confirms this. In a recent survey on performance-enhanced fabrics, 61 percent of shoppers were lured by the wrinkle-free aspect, 47 percent by its stain-resistant quality, and 38 percent for the adjustable waistbands.[6] Only when shoppers have found the features they want will they add additional items to their shopping bags. The challenge, then, is for retailers (and fashion editors and stylists) to demonstrate the relationship between one's clothes, one's lifestyle, and the prevailing trends.

A truly successful merchandise mix will combine tried-and-true basics—such as Levi's jeans, Lacoste polo shirts, and Hanro T-shirts—with more fashion-forward goods, such as Yves Saint-Laurent sportcoats, Paul Smith dress shirts, or Neil Barrett pants. It's a simple approach, but one that, at least in the United States, has been overlooked: teach the customer about "style"—often loosely defined as the mixing and matching of fabrics, silhouettes, designers, colors, and accessories—to create a look that expresses the customer's own individuality.

For retailers, putting such a philosophy of merchandise buying into effect is one of the great opportunities in American menswear retailing. The blending of merchandise visually and in terms of assortment divisions is certain to drive sales and more aggressively educate and inspire a male customer who is already seeking a more individual sense of style. This approach also gives a much sharper and clearer indication of a store's point of view—something men want to know before they walk in the door (unlike women, who like to explore). Retail stores can display their offerings in a variety of ways to tell a unique story about the customer, the store, and the products it has chosen to carry. Together, these give the store a distinct personality and point of view. A man becomes branded when he subscribes to the store's philosophy, trusting its vision and embracing the style it has offered him.

With regard to visual merchandising, why confine it to clothes alone? Why not include lifestyle elements drawn from technology, art, books, and home furnishings? A men's store should be less about stacks of shirts and more about the potential customer and how he lives—or *wishes* he lived. It should display an astutely selected combination of objects that together give context to the man and the world in which he aspires to live. Thus, the act of shopping becomes an occasion for discovery, education, and excitement. A great retail environment satisfies multiple needs on multiple levels. In the next chapter, we'll look at some examples.

Chapter 8: The Take-Away

A successful retailer needs to convey a strong story or point of view. All too often, customers receive confusing messages and the merchandise focus appears random and insincere. So-called premium sportswear has done much to bring a new awareness of classic sportswear and wardrobe foundations. Brand blending, both with visual merchandising and assortment divisions, gives a sharper indication of a store's point of view and clearly illustrates to men the elements of style. A man becomes branded when he subscribes to the store's philosophy, trusting its vision and embracing the style it has offered him.

CHAPTER NINE

The Power of Retail Design

Research on store design and shopper psychology fills end-less volumes, but most research is on how women shop; men are largely ignored. Male shopping patterns can appear mysterious because men do not always fit a recognizable behav-ioral template, especially when they enter a store. When men go shopping, they want the same thing women want: to escape, to dream, to imagine how something can transform their lives, be it a computer, a car, or a suit. The challenge is that men are only just now daring to discover how great clothes can transform them. For men, clothes are still only one part of the big picture, but when clothes are displayed with other lifestyle goods, the picture gains focus. The "lifestyle" approach, an increasingly ubiquitous strategy for luxury retailers, is critical to how menswear should be presented.

Here, let me mention a great pioneer who combined supe-rior merchandise and meticulous editing. Design Research (or "D/R," as fans tended to call it), was a store with outlets in Los Angeles, California, and Hyannis and Cambridge, Massachusetts. From the 1950s through the '60s, D/R's philosophy was to sell contemporary clothing, high-design furniture, and one-of-a-kind accessories in a setting that was like stepping into a trendsetter's stylish home. Gordon Segal,

founder and CEO of Crate and Barrel, credits D/R with helping him understand that "people want to look at merchandise
in lifestyle settings."[1]

What makes D/R an influence even today is its use of multiple design and merchandising features to create a brand that
resonates with customers. The *New York Times* described enter-
ing its Cambridge, Massachusetts, headquarters as an experience of "romance, sociability, sensory pleasure, and human
delight...you realized you were going to live with a different
value system."[2] The building itself was testament to what lay
within, a "cut jewel"; it "was intended as an example of the kind
of good design you'd find in the household articles inside: simple
but well and honestly crafted." This was thorough retail branding at its finest. Before they even entered Design Research's
doors, consumers were given a table of contents, as it were, of
the experience that awaited them within. In short, D/R created a store that had an instantly discernible point of view, with
European furniture, colorful textiles, modern housewares, and
avant-garde clothing. To shop there felt special and allowed a
customer to "penetrate the wall of anonymity."[3]

That could easily describe the desires of the American
customer of today, in a culture where everyone so desperately seeks to be stylish, in a unique way. Moss (in New
York's SoHo) is a twenty-first-century version of D/R, with
an equally eclectic and lofty collection of curated goods. As
their Web site states, "The furniture and objects offered at
the shop deliberately blur the distinctions between production and craft, between industry and art, and more recently,
between industrial and decorative arts. One may find, for
instance, a Hella Jongerius embroidered ceramic pot next to

Tune In, Turn On, Pop Up:
Guerrilla Retail Is Alive and Well

Pop-up stores give customers a totally different experience from the carefully executed store designs of major retailers. These temporary shops create a sense of urgency and performance and allow a retailer to try new merchandising strategies. "This approach 'eventizes' shopping," says a brand agent from Creative Artists Agency. "Young people are taking their cues from their friends, and less and less from established channels like fashion magazines and mass advertising."[5] The fashion cycle is moving so fast that the stores that house the designs need to reflect the same energy. Stores in Japan and Europe are increasingly experimenting with environments that change with practically every store shipment and give the impression of freshness and flux. Lighting changes, movable walls, and other features give stores an organic fluidity that helps set the stage for the merchandise and makes the shopping experience dynamic and exciting.

The success of pop-up retailing resides in the fact that it is casual and approachable, and its limited lifetime says, "Get it while you can."

Comme Des Garçons, for example, was one of the first to experiment with the low-tech approach to retail. It took a former bookstore on the outskirts of central Berlin and made only minor changes to transform it into a pop-up store. In fact, Comme des Garçons only spent $2,500 and didn't even bother taking the old name off the window. To publicize the shop, they put up 600 posters; the rest was simply word of mouth.

At the 2008 Salone Di Mobile in Milan, there were two very different pop-up store concepts that received plenty of attention. Charles & Marie, the San Francisco-based distributor specializing in one-offs and limited editions of home

A Louis Vuitton store features a Comme des Garçons pop-up concept.

accessories and gift items, set up shop for only five days in an empty thrift store in the heart of Milan's Tortona district. The tiny pop-up store was consistently packed with people drawn not only to the merchandise but to its nonconformist, low-profile style.

Meanwhile, across town, corporate beauty brand Nivea installed a portable pop-up store shaped like a doughnut, which offered skin consultations, hair styling services, and a range of skin care products. Vintage bicycles painted electric blue were chained to posts on streets leading up to the shop for a signage concept that doubled as installation art. At the entrance to the store, a tall, handsome model dressed as a security guard stood sentry next to a giant digital clock that ticked off the minutes before the store would fold up and disappear. Beidersdorf AG, Nivea's parent company, says it plans to continue experimenting with its pop-up concept in other cities in Europe.

PHOTO COURTESY OF BIEDERSDORF

Nivea's pop-up experience in Milan.

The energy of a pop-up store is precisely what makes Apple flagships the benchmark for retail success. They've created a similar sense of excitement, freshness, and education that has not been duplicated. Increasingly, when companies come to brand strategists like myself, one of the case studies that always resonate with them is an Apple store. "Their quest is to create the ultimate shopping experience," says NPD's Marshal Cohen. "[It's a] a place for you to 'shop,' learn how to use the product, learn what you can buy to enhance your product... and most importantly, a place to come to feel comfortable, to bond with the brand.... [There's] no pressure to purchase, just a wholesome learning and entertaining environment."

a stainless steel Fisher space pen next to an Edra pink leather Flap sofa. The intention is to force a view of each piece based on the context of its presentation rather than its function or material."[4]

A well-designed environment has the power to give customers a feeling that they are transcending their current selves and becoming someone else—someone more interesting, more attractive, and more worldly—by virtue of the objects that surround them. Ralph Lauren was the first designer to understand this and capitalize on the flagship store as brand storyteller. Today, it is common practice. Consider that at the turn of the century, the department store was a destination as much for its design as for the goods it offered. But somewhere along the way, store design lost its way. Should it overpower the customer, making him or her feel insignificant (Prada's over-designed SoHo flagship is one example of this approach)? Should it attempt to please everyone, making the customer experience uninspired and perfunctory (the midmarket department store excels at this). Or, finally, should it intimidate as do so many designer boutiques?

Today, it is the luxury brands that have set the tone for store design, with sparkling showplaces that generally leave customers feeling as cold as the terrazzo marble and brass fixtures. As designer Paul Smith said, the result is that "all the same streets have the same stores with the same window dressing."[6] Smith knows a thing or two about innovative store design. His stores nod in the direction of the classic English gentleman's store, with the additional charm of vintage toys, books, and found objects. Smith continues to display an authenticity that speaks to an ever-growing customer base, and he has expanded his creative savvy into other parts of the market.

Times have indeed changed, as the *New York Times* astutely noted when Tom Ford bid farewell to Gucci: "Gucci's rise in the 1990s was due to Mr. Ford's ability to read cultural signs and tap into them, with a head-to-toe look that flaunted sex and money ... many consumers now seem to want products that express not a brand lifestyle, but rather, their own."[7] This couldn't be more true today. Although Ford has received critical acclaim for his eponymous men's line, his over-the-top dandy looks appeal primarily to the aesthete. Men—and social norms—have a long way to go before styles like Ford's ever become mainstream (which is probably how he wants it).

Courtesy LVMH

The Louis Vuitton flagship in New York City.

The 1990s excess of luxury giants Gucci, Prada, and Louis Vuitton began a trend toward store environments that ultimately intimidate the customer and design approaches that emphasize extravagance, price, and celebrity status. Peter Marino, the king of luxury retail design, has created a design signature with stores that are not unlike private clubs with their plush carpets, VIP lounges, and custom-made furnishings upholstered in rare leathers. Such environments cajole the customer into believing that to buy there is to become—by proxy—a member of a private club. Yet these are not stores that invite one to linger but rather to slink away with one's status purchase. They dictate our behavior and force us to bow at the altar of the brand. As one journalist wrote: "Before cable, before TiVo, we were sit-back consumers, willing to watch what was put before us. Now we want to participate. We once wanted department stores like Bloomingdale's to give us a show. Now we want to be one of the actors."[8] Which is why stores must evolve in the direction of a rich, multisensory experience that puts the customer front and center.

Today, a store needs to do more than just impress and dress. It must invite the customer to interact with the brand and feel that he is the center of attention and interest; the store, a glittering backdrop to his one-man show. I believe the men's retail store has the potential to become the new paradigm, joining sports bars and gyms in becoming a male comfort zone. Men seek an environment that enhances their very being and gives them a product and store experience that elevate their sense of manhood, belonging, and self-respect. They want the world to know they have arrived. The right store can and should provide that feeling.

Retail Synergy: Location, Location, Location—And Strategy

"There but for the grace of God go I" is what many retailers are thinking these days, as former heavy-hitters bite the dust. In the 1990s, themed shopping—retailing masquerading as an amusement park—was popular. The Disney store is a classic example. But in an age of sharper and more highly calibrated methods of retailing, shopping-as-entertainment is a paradigm that has lost its meaning. The closure of ninety-eight Disney stores recently (in the U.S.) was due not simply to an economic downturn but also to an oversaturation of the market and lack of synergy with neighboring tenants.

In an economic downturn, being next door to Tiffany or Saks Fifth Avenue may no longer be an advantage. Retailing synergy, whether in a boom or a bust, is critical to creating a brand and building on the energy of complementary and parallel products. If you look at any successful store, chances are, they've been careful to align themselves with the right neighboring tenants. The tenant mix can determine whether your store will benefit from the right synergy of other merchants. In one city, for instance, a Circuit City opened just below a popular fitness gym. When men were done working out, how could they resist stopping in to see the latest plasma TVs on sale? While many brands plot the right time and place to open a mega-flagship, it's worth considering that small can indeed be beautiful, especially if nearby adjacencies help to enhance your store's profile. Location truly is key, especially for a men's store.

I believe that men generally respond more to neighborhood stores than they do to megaplex shopping malls. No matter how much he may want to shop, the trials of driving out to a mall, parking, and then finding his way into a crowded and noisy mall are simply not at the top of a man's list of how he'd like to spend his free time. The small, local store allows men to casually stop in with little fuss. Lombardi Sports, which I cited in chapter 7, is a good example of a store that has integrated

The Sharper Image brand lost focus, over-anticipated America's desire for meaningless gadgets, and over-saturated the market with stores in high-rent areas.

itself into the local community and feels less complicated. Lombardi's shares the street with several popular bars, coffee shops, and a gym.

And then there are some brands that lost their mojo because they became redundant on the retail playing field. The Sharper Image brand became irrelevant not only because of its high-profile debacle with an air purifier manufacturer (resulting in a class-action lawsuit and a large inventory of unsold products) but also because of an oversaturation of the market. With shops located in just about every airport, the store became "gadget central" rather than a place for innovative products. The brand ceased to be relevant in a world where new technology moves so fast that by the time it is displayed in a store it's already being discounted online or at Best Buy. The Sharper Image, once every guy's favorite place to browse and play, became hopelessly outdated—even kitsch. The brand got lost in a time warp that banked on the wrong products and became a symbol of the past rather than the future.

The other mistake brands can make is greed. They see an empty space and think more stores equal more profit. That was certainly the case with Starbucks, and they've paid the price. In 2008 they scaled back considerably in favor of quality over quantity and a return to their roots. Retailers who have strong online or catalog followings should strategically use their customer data to target where to open their next store. That's what Talbots did. "We have a proven formula in which we take our catalog data to tell where our customers are and what they're buying," says a brand spokesperson. "Hypothetically, if we did $150,000 in catalog sales in a particular area last year, we know we can put a store there and do $1 million–$1.5 million in retail sales."[9]

Distance is another critical factor, and men are no less immune to it than women. A store has to be an obvious destination, whether it's on his way to getting coffee on a Sunday afternoon or conveniently located near his office or transit station. How many times have you popped into a store because it was "on your way"? That's why. Men look for the shortest route to their destination and will visit a store only if it's clear that it has something to offer and won't take them too far off schedule from what they need to do. Choosing a retail location *is* about location, but it's also about balancing that location with retail synergy, the right product for that location, and a strong demographic understanding of the people who live and shop there.

Chapter 9: The Take-Away

Retailers that take a lifestyle approach to store design and pro-gramming are more effectively positioned to gain customer trust and loyalty. The overdesigned concept stores created by luxury retailers like Gucci and Prada lack warmth and do not invite the customer to interact with the brand in a meaningful way. A man seeks places that offer compelling and emotional experiences that enhance his sense of manhood, belonging, and self-respect. Store location is critical. No matter how origi-nal a concept might be, there must be synergy with the store's adjacencies. A careful evaluation of the site is important in ensuring that men can easily find the store and relate easily to the product and that other merchants in the area have comple-mentary client bases that will bring value and synergy to the retail location.

CHAPTER TEN
Using Technology to Enhance the Men's Retail Experience

Innovation in retail technology is paving the way toward giving customers greater control and information in making purchase decisions, and creating the foundation for an *immersive* retailing experience. An immersive experience is one that connects with shoppers on an emotional level using tools that give them greater control and connection with their shopping experience. Interactive mirrors, 3-D scanners, and even holographic sales assistants are fast becoming part of the retail landscape and enhancing how fashion brands respond to the competition—but are they right for your store?

The answer lies in how and when that technology is used. Immersive technology can only enhance what already exists in your customer service strategy. But in the case of how shoppers use a fitting room, there are opportunities worth considering. Fitting rooms can be difficult for some stores to manage because sales associates often juggle more than one customer at a time. It's a scenario many of us are familiar with: you try on several items, perhaps in two different sizes, and you can't decide which to buy, or maybe no one is around to help you get another size. These are a few of the reasons men

An example of touch-responsive technology (used by Infiniti) that allows the user to customize their information.

hate shopping. Technology research firm PARC developed "responsive" mirrors that allow shoppers to simultaneously see pictures of themselves in all the clothing items they've tried on, all in the privacy of the fitting room. Prada has already begun using responsive mirrors in its Beverly Hills stores and in its SoHo flagship.

Meanwhile, Japanese retailer Mitsukoshi was one of the first to test the concept of an "intelligent fitting room," whereby customers check available sizes and styles of the items they are trying on through technology that is installed in the fitting room. Does that compromise the opportunity for sales associates to personally connect with customers? Yes, but as many retailers know, consistency in customer service is a constant battle.

New technologies can potentially help supplement poor customer service with self-service; however, I would proceed with extreme caution: technology is inherently impersonal and dispassionate—poison for a store experience. But shoppers are generally receptive to gizmos when they serve to complement a team of attentive sales associates. Consider also that in a recent survey, 73 percent of shoppers said that they anticipate using concepts such as interactive touch screens to communicate with sales associates by 2015, while half look forward to 3-D body scanning and interactive dressing room mirrors.[1]

Men generally lack confidence in making what they perceive as a "risky" fashion decision. If they are looking to buy jeans, they're not likely to leave with other unforeseen purchases unless they have received approval from someone they trust. Social retailing systems allow shoppers to record video of themselves wearing merchandise and then share those images with friends through email or a proprietary Web site—all from the dressing room. The system, developed by IconNicholson, features an interactive mirror and Webcam in the fitting room. Such a concept might be more readily accepted by teenagers and women than by men, but don't discount it too quickly: with the surge in social networking sites (MySpace, Friendster, Twitter, and Facebook, to name a few), it won't be long before everyone is sharing even the most mundane details of their lives.

It's worth remembering, though, that none of this technology comes cheap: for instance, scanners that can detect a customer's size can cost up to $75,000 each, and maintenance of such systems is expensive but important because there is nothing that frustrates a customer more than broken equipment. But creating a great fitting room experience doesn't have to break the bank. The basics are simple: fitting rooms should be as large as possible, with optimum lighting, plenty of undistorted mirrors, and maybe even some simple refreshments.

What man wouldn't enjoy finding a bucket of cold beer waiting in his fitting room? In the end, a well-managed store should always take full advantage of its fitting rooms to close the deal. Says Ken Nisch, chairman of retail consulting firm JGA, "It provides an unencumbered way to talk with customers about the brand and engage and interact with them beyond the sales floor."[1]

"As Seen on TV": In-Store Retailtainment

London's wildly popular Topman store (an offshoot of Topshop) is a model for fast fashion at its best. The store is a destination for the eighteen- to twenty-four-year-old (and older customers as well) that offers special events, limited-edition fashion items, a hair salon, and even live music performances. Multimedia in the form of on-site Internet stations and plasma TVs offer a smorgasbord of fashion information; in fact, at one time the store even had its own on-camera personalities who hosted in-store fashion shows. Tesco PLC, Britain's biggest supermarket chain, experimented with using television advertising in 300 of its stores,[2] while in the United States, Wal-Mart Stores, Inc., has done the same. Wal-Mart TV has over 125,000 screens in about 3,100 of the brand's 4,022 U.S. stores. They claim that an estimated 127 million shoppers per week are watching the proprietary network. Wal-Mart's system—operated by Premier Retail Networks—shows news, weather, and entertainment interspersed with paid advertising.[3] The idea is simple: provide entertainment, information, and advertising for products and services available in the store while simultaneously capitalizing on a captive audience. Premier Retail Networks has also run

Korean VJ Jigeng Kim hosts a live fashion program in the in-store television studio at Avenuel department store in Seoul, Korea. The programming helps market the store's brands and lifestyle image.

in-store TV networks for Best Buy Co. and claims an estimated viewership of more than 185 million people a month. Even smaller boutique stores are testing out the potential. Oslo's, a boutique men's store in Seattle (featured in chapter 7) has hired multimedia marketing firm Retail Entertainment Design (RED) to create custom collections of music videos geared specifically toward the brands they sell.

While some question whether the proprietary in-store television concept pays off in comparison to traditional banner advertising and the like, it can be argued that the TV system—if sophisticated enough—can become a respected "voice" for the brand. I developed an in-store television concept for a major department store retailer in Korea, with a glass-walled studio space that allowed shoppers to watch and participate in the action. We hired a top male model as the on-camera personality and he anchored a range of MTV-style programming, from live interviews with designers to lifestyle segments on food, cars, and of course, fashion. The concept helped to position the store as a luxury lifestyle authority. The programming was not only broadcast throughout the store but also on jumbo screens on the façade of the building and on the in-room television network of the company's hotel partner. An estimated 13 million people a month watched this programming, whether while sitting in their cars waiting for the light to change, as visitors staying in the hotel, or as shoppers in the store.

I believe there is great potential in creating stylish broadcast and Internet content that amplifies the personality of a store and communicates just-in-time messaging about fashion trends, new merchandise, and in-store events and activities, all with a distinct point of view.

Online Retailing: Men Are Just A Click Away

Many brick-and-mortar store brands have only recently taken their online identities seriously. But a brand's online identity is just as important as the actual store itself. An online identity acts as a 24-hour billboard to the brand and, when designed properly, can substantially drive sales and awareness. It's estimated that U.S. online shoppers will double to 132 million in the next five years, and men have emerged as the most active group, contributing to over half of all sales.

Hard to believe? According to NPD, men's purchase of online apparel rose 4.4 percent or $57.2 billion between 2007 and 2008, compared to only a 1.1 percent increase with women. In another 2008 survey of 1,608 online consumers, 16 percent of men (versus 10 percent of women) planned to spend between $500 and $1,000. Even more telling is the fact that 68 percent of men versus 57 percent of women say they are "as comfortable buying online as in person."[4] What's more, men typically don't return items; in fact, they return less than 10 percent of overall purchases. Information like this is why Neiman Marcus didn't waste any time launching a new Web site presence with an enhanced presentation of men's merchandise designed to get their attention. Before, the site was geared almost exclusively toward women who made purchases for men. From sneakers to stereos, shopping online is not only convenient for men, but it also offers precisely what the store experience often does not: fast and reliable price comparison, convenience, and clear, concise product information.

But Web sites designed for a male target audience still need careful consideration. Where women like to browse and often roam through a Web site (and easily refine their searches with multiple search terms to find what they want), men just want to buy what they're looking for as quickly and easily as possible. Men shop by category, and once they've found what they're looking for, they generally won't dig much more deeply into a site's offering. That's why many sites are adding features such as side columns near the checkout that feature suggested pairing items so men can see other merchandise that might complement a purchase before they complete their payments.

Younger demographics (people in their late teens and early twenties) are showing remarkable savvy in navigating Web sites, and with the popularity of social networking sites, shopping and browsing online has now become a group activity. "Most young people in their twenties are getting all their content on the Internet," says Andrew Hargadon, associate professor at the Graduate School of Management at UC Davis and author of *How Breakthroughs Happen: The Surprising Truth About How Companies Innovate.* "They're finding more of their needs satisfied online. It's become a place where they can not only exchange ideas, but also make decisions about what to buy."[5] In the online world, shoppers can not only compare prices and product ratings, but also discuss the benefits of a product in chat rooms and with friends. What results are real-time user testimonials that can influence buying decisions, creating an altogether different experience from shopping alone in a store. But many retailers continue to see their online brand identity as merely a virtual storefront rather than as an opportunity to meaningfully connect with the customer. Chat rooms, fan sites, and fashion blogs are just a few places where retailers can develop a client base and provide customized information. Says Hargadon, "Retailers should really embrace the online world

The MySpace Fashion Internet channel is an online community dedicated to fashion lovers that allows them to immerse themselves in a world of fashion obsessives and (not so coincidentally) allows them to shop as well.

and try to create their own online communities. Consumers are becoming more accustomed to a fair amount of meaning associated with a product, and Internet communities give producers and retailers real user experience and feedback. It's also where they can provide a deeper meaning behind the product than they might be able to in a store."

In 2007, MySpace launched the MySpace Fashion Channel, a subcommunity that allows users to connect with brands, designers, and fashion world celebrities. Designed like an online magazine, the site lets ordinary people talk about their fashion opinions. "If you're an apparel or fashion marketer, MySpace Fashion will give you a focus group to test your product and receive feedback from your core user," says Todd Dufour, director of strategic partnerships at MySpace.[6] In turn, designers get a direct communications line to the consumer that keeps them right on the pulse. The site makes heavy use of streaming video from fashion shows and parties, which means there is almost no downtime in keeping consumers on the cutting edge of new collections. But at the time of this writing, MySpace is still strongly slanted toward women and it's hard to tell if a male audience will catch on.

Like a brick-and-mortar store, the true spirit of an online presence should always be about service. The customer's first concern is to navigate as quickly as possible to the items that interest him or her and make a purchase. But what if the customer could actually see how an item might look when they put it on? Enter My Virtual Model, Inc., a Canadian firm that has designed virtual identity platforms for clients such as H&M, Adidas, and Levi's. Like a virtual avatar, customers create their own 3-D persona online with a program called BrandME, then shop for clothes from participating merchants. While still a long way off from becoming the norm, the prospect of shopping with a virtual identity offers an intriguing look at the evolution of the personalized online shopping experience, which could certainly have potential for the male customer.

But even if you don't decide to invest in a virtual avatar component for your site, it's still important to keep the online store as fresh and exciting as the brick-and-mortar one. In the same way that a retailer invests in new fixtures, lighting, and visual merchandising, an online presence needs the same image refreshment. "While it may be accounted for differently, you have to spend capital to keep online stores shipshape," says Alex Bolen, chief executive officer for Oscar de la Renta. "It's a different expense, different kinds of things, but very analogous to brick-and-mortar stores.... You've got to keep the customer experience new and fresh."[7] Video content is becoming increasingly critical to staying competitive, and brands like Neiman Marcus, Saks Fifth Avenue, and Net-a-porter.com are using video to present merchandise to its best advantage and, most importantly, to drive sales. Exclusive features such as designer interviews and live fashion shows are just one way that brands bring customers closer to the products they sell.

Moosejaw Mountaineering, Inc., is an outdoor sporting equipment store based in Madison Heights, Michigan, with seven stores throughout Michigan and Chicago. The company has invested in a host of IBM software and hardware products to increase the performance and capability of their Web site. Here, customers can access customer reviews and special promotions and engage with a community of outdoor enthusiasts with social commerce features that give products greater visibility and integrity. A customer, for example, can actually get feedback on a tent they want to buy for a trip up Mount Everest. "We are on the verge of truly blurring the lines between Web, retail, mobile, catalog, call center, and kiosk," says Jeffrey Wolke, CEO of Moosejaw, Inc. "It's taking the best of each channel and making it possible across all channels."[8] In store, customers can use the exact same features they're familiar with online—choose, pay, and ship.

No matter how deep a brand plans to go with online retailing, the goal should always be to make the real and virtual store equally inspiring and exciting, and completely consistent with the overarching brand spirit, message, and tone.

The Cardinal Rules for a Successful Men's Retail Web Site

The following are pretty much mandatory for a Web site that caters to a predominantly male audience, especially if the goal is to get them to shop.

1) *Refresh your "front window" or homepage often, and make it easy to navigate.* Your homepage should be clean and simple with timely messaging about key items. Allow men to skip any intro animations and don't make them search for links to category pages.

2) *Put all of your products (or as many as you can fit) on one page.* Men shop in the cyber world the same as they do in a store. They want to get what they need first, and then they might browse.

3) *Use optimized technology to speed page loading and scrolling functions.* NeimanMarcus.com, for instance, lets you see fifty-two ties at once and see the price and designer of each simply by holding the mouse over the item.

4) *When in doubt, let them "View All."* Men don't want to click through pages. Let them see all the pants in stock, then let them decide if they want to narrow their selection by color, style, or designer.

Chapter 10: The Take-Away

Every retailer should explore new and emerging technology, whether for in store or online. Interactive features for fitting rooms can increase total purchases and give men greater insight and control over what they buy. But technology shouldn't replace actual human interaction. Store staff is still a brand's most important asset. Television and multimedia can speak to the customer in places where the staff can't. Branded video content that plays in fitting rooms, elevator lobbies, and other areas brings customized entertainment and information to the customer experience. An online presence is critical to any store or brand and is generally a low-cost marketing opportunity that, if maintained properly, can quantifiably increase brand awareness. Men have emerged as the leading demographic when it comes to shopping online, which is why brands should develop long term strategies to bank on e-tailing opportunities. Web design should include software platforms that optimize the user experience so that shopping is fast and easy.

CHAPTER ELEVEN

Setting the Stage: Activating the Store

L ike their female counterparts, men are looking for places that satisfy multiple desires and needs. In chapter 5, we examined several environments where men typically feel comfortable: fitness clubs, sports bars, strip clubs, and electronics stores. There is no reason why a men's store cannot—or should not—incorporate features, textures, and flourishes from all of these places.

The hospitality industry offers important insights on what it means to provide special services and "extras" in order to make a hotel or resort both memorable and practical. Even the airline industry has jumped into the hospitality game—just take a look at their first-class and business lounges. Recently, Virgin Airlines blew away the competition. The Virgin Clubhouse at Kennedy Airport features two shower rooms, fully stocked refrigerators, and wireless Internet service. The lounge also serves freshly prepared meals so travelers can get to sleep immediately after boarding. For preflight rest, the lounge features an alcove with daybeds, iPod digital music players, and a constantly updated range of music. Private rooms add to this home-away-from-home atmosphere, and a sexy dash of: "are you really in there alone?" It's important to keep in mind that these are environments that cater largely to men, who still make up the lion's share of business travelers. Airlines have made an art out of making men feel like they just got a promotion and the key to the executive washroom.

A store could (and should) offer many of the same benefits that an airline offers its premium business class members. Since we now know that men shop with the goals of self-enhancement and entertainment—and that most stores make shopping a chore and largely uninspiring—then it only stands to reason that the audience is there but the show's a bore.

So what would the ideal store look like? Here's how I imagine it:

• *An Edited Assortment of "Must Have" Clothes*

As I mentioned earlier, a curated assortment of merchandise is what gives a store its point of view and its appeal. One must, of course, begin with a firm foundation, even if there are some flights of fancy. Imagine a store whose carefully selected range of merchandise includes timeless classics such as Levi's jeans, BVD or Hanro underwear, Macintosh raincoats, etc. On the other end of the spectrum we might find great designer suits, sportswear, and specialty items from the world's leading designers. These clothes would be presented as if in a man's own closet, blended together regardless of price point, but assembled with an eye for taste and style (Dover Street Market in London is one example of a store that employs this approach). Sales associates (or consultants), always available but not obtrusive, would present choices, using the "good, better, best" philosophy by indicating the "best of" at each price point and deftly editing selections for the customer.

- *An Interactive Technology Area*

A section set slightly apart would be a zone where men can see and try the latest in new technology, from PDAs to computers, from cellular phones to digital video and gaming gear. Customers might even be able to take merchandise home for a "test drive." Each Saturday, the store would feature free demonstrations and workshops, in much the same way that Apple stores offer "tips and tricks" for their software platforms and computers.

- *An Exhibition Space*

In a store that is more than a store, a public exhibition space could offer a broad range of exhibits: concept cars, photography, vintage books (first editions of James Bond), pop culture (first-generation video gaming), vintage toys and T-shirts, and so on. There might even be special events associated with the exhibits. Such displays not only attract the general public, among whom, of course, are potential customers, but also serve to reinforce the store's positioning as a men's environment: for men, about men, but, like a sports bar, a place where women also are welcome.

- *A Lounge Bar*

Ideally, the lounge bar would include a dedicated street-level entrance. By day, the lounge could be a place to simply hang out, meet friends, read, or watch sports. At night, after the store itself has closed, the space would change. Men and women could meet with friends over drinks in a more stylish version of a sports bar, the nexus of where *Cheers* and the Playboy Club meet. There might even be sleeping "pods" where customers could relax and nap. Rather than being completely closed off from the retail portion of the store, the lounge bar might feature attractive displays that serve as dramatic showcases for new merchandise.

• *A Barbershop/Grooming Spa*

Here we'd take a page from the classic American barbershop, with some added attractions. Imagine widescreen TVs, spa services, and a pharmacy that sells both grooming supplies and a variety of sexual aids such as condoms, lubricants, and a range of fun, tongue-in-cheek sex toys (inflatable doll, anyone?).

• *A Laundry Service and Tailoring Center*

For the man in a hurry (or the man who is simply lazy), a full-service laundry and tailoring shop will be provided, with pick-up and delivery services.

Additional services might include a concierge with the ability to obtain premium tickets for concerts and organize excursions to ski resorts, river rafting, and other sports-related events. This reinforces the concept of the store as a community center and clubhouse. (Note: any or all additional store features—bar, barbershop, laundry center—could be outsourced or given over to a leased tenant. However, great care would have to be taken to ensure that the tenant's style is consistent with the store's brand identity.) The store might even feature a premium membership card that would allow clients to earn points toward goods and services in the store's barbershop or bar or discounts toward merchandise—something that is already in practice at Neiman Marcus and some other specialty retailers.

Chapter 11: The Take-Away

A store should take a strategic approach to how it programs its men's offering, whether it be a department store or a local boutique. When possible, the store should present itself as being instinctively attuned to a man's array of interests and concerns. Rather than being simply a place to buy clothes, a store can and should offer other programs such as exhibitions, interactive technology, bars or hospitality zones, and even barbershops and laundry services. Like a gentleman's club, a men's store becomes a kind of clubhouse for self-evolution, activity, and discovery.

CHAPTER TWELVE
The Store as Town Square: A Toolbox for Creating Customer Community

Today's store relies on design, regardless of what it is offering for sale. Once upon a time, the opposite was true. A store had no real design. It consisted of rows of showcases and tables heaped with merchandise. Now, a store is not merely designed; its layout is the object of intensive study and research. Experts emphasize an intuitive "user journey" and are constantly exploring new ways to communicate the brand experience through that journey as well as through the key touchpoints of product and service interaction. Writes brand designer Marc Gobé, "The most important thing is that a retail concept be 'people oriented' and that its execution be well designed. Design indeed transcends technology—it is about ideas that you can see—and it can be very powerful in creating a total brand experience at the retail level, whether through high-tech or low-tech solutions."[1]

The most successful and authentic brand experience is one that feels organic and appears to be activated by the user. A great store, far from being blatantly orchestrated (think theme restaurants), does not simply aim to sell the product, but rather to establish an emotional significance that resonates with the individual's sense of self and desire to believe in something more inspiring than the objects he came to buy.

It's a concept that's paid off in many instances. Consider REI, Inc., who hired global design firm Gensler to design a new 42,000-square-foot flagship experience for their Boulder,

The REI, Inc., flagship experience in Boulder, Colorado, took its existing fanatical customer base and gave it a "community center" focused on service, product knowledge, and outdoor lifestyle.

Colorado, store in 2007. Dean Iwata, REI's director of store development, says, "The objective of our prototype store was to envision what REI stores would look and function like in the future, with a special focus on the environment and the community."[2] The Boulder store features a central hub where workshops, demonstrations, and other activities promote interaction and create an animated atmosphere. REI is a good example of what happens when a store offers a gathering place that communicates its brand message to a captive audience through an engaging and interactive in-store experience.

The branded community experience is proof that it is possible to replace the town square, the front porch, or the small-town coffee shop and make it a meaningful part of the customer experience. Starbucks took ownership of the traditional coffee shop and found a way to respond to the people's need for a "third place" (Oldenberg, 1989) beyond their home or workplace. They elevated it and branded it (think soft seating, designer coffee drinks, and proprietary music), which caused an entire community to form around the brand. Taking that idea one step further is Borders, where customers sit for hours and read unpaid-for books and magazines. In a new prototype store in Ann Arbor, Michigan, Borders has pushed even further to enhance the browsing experience with a range of digital and Internet offerings that turns the bookstore into so much more. This Borders store bridges the online world and the real one with a "digital center" where customers can do everything from download music and books to print photos, and even publish their own books. They can also explore their family tree, thanks to a partnership with Ancestry.com, and then turn their discoveries into a book. Once again, it's not so much about the

The Borders flagship in Ann Arbor, Michigan. The store has elevated and reformatted the retail bookstore experience to include a "digital center" where customers can print pictures, research their family trees, and even self-publish books.

PHOTO COURTESY LASZLO REGOS

purchase as it is about building a sense of community and discovery. The digital zone is completely self-service, but Borders also provides specially trained staff to help the non-tech-savvy customer.[3] How, you may ask, does this kind of business practice actually contribute to the bottom line—especially if no one seems to be buying anything? It works because customers

THE STORE AS TOWN SQUARE: A TOOLBOX FOR CREATING CUSTOMER COMMUNITY

are willing to part with their money if a store allows them to become active consumers, apparently getting something free in a place that respects their deepest human needs (such as the need for community in a capitalistic, consumer-driven society). In today's world, few things are more seductive or conducive to sales.

With an increase in rootless populations and a decrease in public space, there is a growing need among young, single, urban workers to find a place to go. Stores and public spaces with café environments are filling a vacuum. Consider that when the Rem Koolhaas-designed Seattle Library opened, it quickly became as much a social gathering hub as a public library. On any given day, its Internet zones, café, and other open spaces are buzzing with activity. Critics say the building lacks cohesiveness with the outside world, turning inward instead of outward. But at its core, it does what an urban public space is meant to do: it brings people together.

Retail—for better or for worse—has the power to co-opt the very real need for a safe, clean, and pleasant public space and use it as a strategic tool for building consumer trust and confidence, and yes, even generating sales.

Looking for Love: Selling Romance to Men

Single men and women in large urban cities are finding it harder and harder to find a partner. About 40 percent of U.S. adults are unmarried—up from 28 percent in 1970—which means big business for dating services. It's estimated that such companies earn roughly $1 billion a year in business in the U.S. alone. Online dating services have boomed in popularity since 2001 and represent nearly 50 percent of the market's value.[4] While online dating has become increasingly accepted as an option for meeting a potential partner, it still has the whiff of desperation. Sites like *www.true.com* seem to be more about finding sex than about finding a partner. Their provocative pop-up ads on Internet sites ask men to "Stop. Stare. Flirt." while videos show scantily clad women who wave, wink, and giggle. But many men are hesitant to sign up for a dating service; as an executive with one such service observes, "a lot of men don't like to go that deep, especially when it's with a stranger." Men now make up about 60 percent of visitors to online personals, where they can maintain a certain level of anonymity. In response to an article about dating services in the *Wall Street Journal*, one reader wrote, "Plain and simple…men hate the thought of resorting to a dating service. Once the guy gets over that hurdle and decides to try a service, the challenge becomes a money issue." Another plaintively said, "Most low-to-mid salary earning women want rich men. I'm not rich… I'm 35 years old, make about $52,000 a year, and am good looking. But I haven't had a date in a year. It's not that easy for guys to meet girls, either."[5]

Such comments suggest another opportunity for a men's store. What if in-house special events became opportunities for busy professional women to meet stylish, single men? Orchestrated singles events would bring a sense of purpose, excitement, and competition to a men's store, giving the male customer ample reason to look good for Lady Luck. In a sense, it would bring dating back to its roots: a real face-to-face interaction instead of the uncertainty of an online dating service.

Chapter 12: The Take-Away

A store that offers opportunities for discovery, community, and camaraderie is better positioned to increase its value in the mind of the male customer. Whether a store employs top-notch technology or takes a simple, grassroots approach to engaging the customer, the most authentic brand experience is one that feels organic and appears to be activated by the user. Brands like REI, Inc., Borders, and even the Seattle Public Library have maximized their potential audiences by offering additional opportunities for the customer to explore and discover a subject, congregate in a comfortable atmosphere, and in the end connect with the brand's core values. In-store multimedia also serves to entertain and inform a customer and has been proven with major retailers such as Wal-Mart. The store-as-town-square is also an opportunity to allow men to connect romantically. Despite the popularity of online dating services, men and women seek meaningful face-to-face meetings, and the right store could potentially offer a forum in which men could meet potential partners.

CHAPTER THIRTEEN

Customer Service: A Store's Recipe for Success

U.S. men's magazines, from *Details* to *GQ*, have taken a fresh approach to their editorial content. Where once they pictured things most men wouldn't be caught dead wearing, it's now all about mentoring men in their sartorial pursuits with simple, clear solutions and proven trend-spotting—"See? Guys really *are* wearing it!" The now-defunct *Cargo* magazine was the first to experiment with gimmicks once found only in women's magazines like *Lucky*: things like stick-on tabs to mark the "must haves." Ariel Foxman, *Cargo*'s former editor-in-chief, says, "It's not about prescribing things you have to buy to be cool or fine-tune your persona, but about providing information and making suggestions so that men can be self-assured in their purchases."[1]

So, if a magazine can offer such a distinct point of view, why can't a store? Maybe because so many stores still haven't figured out that building a great brand, especially a retail menswear brand, is about offering a sincere service experience that goes beyond selling. Where a magazine dictates, a store can dialogue and offer unique, interactive components that create a customized, personal experience. Customer service, then, is the key driver in communicating both the product and the store's distinctive ethos.

Enough cannot be said about the importance of a great sales team and a great customer service program. Actually, a lot has been said, but people still aren't listening. Advocates continue to underscore its relevance in building a brand. In *The Marketing Power of Emotion,* John O'Shaughnessy and Nicholas Jackson O'Shaughnessy write, "Brand images can evoke emotional bonding with the customer, creating trust and arousing loyalty."[2] For that to happen, though, customers must first establish a bond with the store in a meaningful way, and this is why the employee is so critical to making that happen. While customer surveys can help retailers to understand a shopper's motivations, what they overlook, particularly in regard to the men's market, is that "satisfactory" tends to merely mean "no serious complaints." This is unacceptable if we believe in the axiom that to successfully brand the man there must be a deeper emotional connection—this is the goal if a store is to secure a loyal customer. And there is no more challenging (or more loyal) customer than a man, once a meaningful connection has been established.

Consider again the Apple store. Like many successful brands, Apple invests serious time and money in reviewing and grooming store employees. Says one analyst, "Apple is able to employ quirky people who fit their own culture... for the first time, it is fun to interface with someone who you hope never dates your daughter."[3] Mac Specialists generally come to the brand with an existing knowledge of the products—something not always found at a Best Buy, where employees can't possibly have the depth of experience necessary to sell so many brands.

Apple goes to considerable lengths to hire the right employees for its stores. "Mac Specialists" are ambassadors to the Apple brand.

When customers go to the "Genius Bar," they feel confident that the staff not only know what they're doing, but also that they genuinely enjoy themselves and believe in the product. They are true brand ambassadors.

In research by Deloitte Consulting, "customer-centric" companies are 60 percent more profitable than those that are not, and they have lower overall operating costs as well. Deloitte defines customer-centrism as "a systematic process that sets objectives for customer loyalty and retention, and then tracks performance towards these goals."[5] It is perhaps the most vital factor in positioning any store but, surprisingly, it continues to be consistently overlooked, even though bookstores brim with titles that offer solutions to invigorating employee performance. Titles like *All Business is Show Business, The Power of Nice, Customer Satisfaction is Worthless But Customer Loyalty is Priceless,* and *How to Win Customers and Keep Them for Life* (proof that if you ever plan to write one of these books, you should make sure the title is long enough to cover the entire book jacket). Yet to the casual shopper, customer service can appear to depend on how much one is willing to spend—the more one spends, the better the service. And that's on a good day, because sometimes not even that makes any difference. I have spoken to many men who claim salespeople are "sizing up" their appearance and trying to guess their relative value with regard to making a sale. This discrimination is, alas, common practice in countless stores, from luxury to mass.

This is why I use the hospitality industry as a benchmark for developing almost any retail customer-service component. A hotel's goal is certainly about selling rooms, but the bottom line is about serving the customer regardless of his or her social status or brand of shoes. Conrad Hilton was famously one of the first to create a template for customer service that was consistent in each and every hotel bearing his name. Similarly, a great store should be operated like a fine hotel or restaurant. When the customer is treated as graciously as a guest, he or she returns again and again. Staff training is integral to making this happen—ensuring that employees genuinely reflect and enact the standards of the hotel.

A "store that is more than a store" offers a total experience much like that of a great resort hotel, spa, or first-class shipboard cabin. It begins with employees that are the embodiment of the brand and its philosophy and makes for a magical customer experience. It is magical because the factors that compose the experience are invisible and seamless to the untrained eye. But

'The Customer is King':
Nordstrom's Famous Customer Service

TIP **Nº 12**

What should
my socks match?

My shoes?
My shirt?
My tie?

smart clothes
NORDSTROM

clothing
that thinks
like you

It seems there are countless retellings of how Nordstrom took a two-year-old pair of worn-out shoes and gave the customer his money back. Nordstrom's return policy is at once impressive and questionable. How (and why) do they do it? Well, consider that the shoe business is the backbone of Nordstrom's identity in terms of assortment and service. Says Bruce Nordstrom: "I can't think of any other area where you greet the customer, then go back and get merchandise for them and actually kneel on the floor before them and put it on their feet. That's symbolic and service-intensive. That's what retailing is about."[4]

Nordstrom has a reputation for building strong loyalty among its employees, empowering them, and recognizing their achievements. The chain also has some of the most loyal customers of any store in the world. Through a strictly maintained customer service program, Nordstrom manages to retain more than 5 percent of their customer base every year. The reason for its success is relatively simple:

Nordstrom makes customer service one of their core values and empowers frontline employees to do what's necessary to achieve success in service.

While the brand hasn't exactly broken the mold of menswear retailing—it's fairly typical and doesn't bother with bells and whistles—it still makes "service" a priority, even if a man doesn't want to ask for help. At one time, a free-standing rack in the men's suiting department held a series of index cards with answers to men's most commonly asked wardrobe questions: "I used to be able to go casual at work; now I have to dress up. Help!" or, "What should my socks match?" The cards featured a logo with a tag line that read: *Smart clothes . . . clothing that thinks like you.* It was hard to tell how many men actually used the cards, and it's true that, in the end, this counters the importance of one-on-one service. But the cards are an interesting approach to bringing self-help to the sartorially challenged.

in reality they are born of a union of great merchandise, inspiring store design, and knowledgeable, approachable employees who are perfect reflections of that brand. Kenneth Kannady, a CRM consultant, identifies this magic as "the feeling that customers develop about themselves as a result of interacting with a company through its people, products, processes, or services. Empowerment is what differentiates a repeat customer from a loyal customer."[6]

Wilkes Bashford puts it this way: "Ideally, you have a diverse set of staff who satisfy and can communicate with different demographics and personalities. They need to be able to guide the customer and really listen and hear what their needs are. They also need to be sophisticated. A customer wants someone who understands and appreciates their world—even if it's very different from that of the employee."[7]

A sophisticated, empathetic employee can be the intermediary who enables the customer to discover who he can become through the transformative power of clothes. Says Bashford, "Once they experience great tailoring, they see how it frames who they are. A great suit with fine tailoring not only changes how you look but how you feel. Once a man understands that, he's bought into why clothes are so important." The store is a place to experience, imagine, and discover just how clothes can indeed make the man. The sales associate is both guide and accomplice in that situation.

In chapter 4, I featured a case study on men's strip clubs. Take an imaginative leap: what if a men's store had sales associates who were all women? Remember that the majority of men still go shopping with women or entrust their shopping to a woman. With the right female sales associate, a man might feel a greater level of comfort and validation than he would in dealing with a male sales associate. At a designer trunk show, a male customer I observed could barely make eye contact with the salesmen, let alone the male model the store hired to show the season's latest looks. He awkwardly looked at the clothes on the racks, reaching for the familiar basics: jeans, T-shirts, a leather jacket. The one female employee working the floor got him to try on not only the jeans, but some of the new season's more fashion-forward items too. More importantly, he bought. The point being, while many men still trust sales*men* for advice, it's not too far-fetched to envision a store whose "hook" is that it is staffed exclusively by attractive, smart, young, female sales associates who are able to relate in a professional yet mildly flirtatious way to the diffident or inexperienced male customer. Of course, it goes without saying that there's a fine line between an innovative store concept and a Hooters.

Making the Employee a Part of the Brand

No matter how great they are, some men's stores are still subject to the same problems all stores have, including maintaining a superior staff. The retention rate for retail employees is notoriously low, and budget cuts and poor sales have forced many stores to eliminate positions. So how does a store make a lot out of a little? As one senior executive put it, "I can do everything right in marketing—have the right messages, target the right customer, make the right promises—but it is all for naught if the person at the cash register is having a bad day. That's the last impression of my brand that the customer will have."[8] Paul Fitzpatrick, menswear executive vice president and general merchandise manager for Macy's West, says that

getting employees on board is about "reinforcement, reinforcement, reinforcement." I would go even further and suggest that
retailers reinforce the golden rules: 1) acknowledge and listen
to the customer, 2) have the key messages of the season at your
fingertips, and 3) be able to apply them meaningfully to each
individual customer. Fitzpatrick says that Macy's West goes
so far as to quantify customers' responses to their shopping
experiences through a range of data collection; furthermore,
it responds to each and every person's complaint. In addition,
Macy's provide ongoing incentive programs—contests, prizes,
etc.—to encourage high performance from their sales associates.
Nevertheless, Fitzpatrick acknowledges that companies like
Macy's still don't really know how to make the employee a part
of the success of a company, saying that "that's money that's not
well understood … and we don't spend enough on that."

More and more companies are struggling with the question
of how to make employees "brand ambassadors" by giving them
the validation and responsibility of becoming part of the brand.
But success stories do exist. Organizations have developed
programs based on volunteerism, team-building retreats, and
other employee recognition strategies, which have had a proven
effect on both staff retention and the quality of customer service. Alan J. Fuerstman, chief executive of Montage Hotels and
Resorts, says the investment in staff training can never be over-
emphasized. "We are very big on offering all employees extra-
curricular educational opportunities that can be applied in or
out of our hotel. We sponsor leadership trainings based on *The
Seven Habits of Highly Effective People.*" Montage employees
also receive intensive training in "Listening and Language" and
a class called "Wow"—which they define as a "spontaneous,
personal gesture."[9]

As a consultant for Louis Vuitton in South Korea, I dealt first hand with some of the troubling scenarios that can afflict even a major luxury brand. At the time, the Korean Louis Vuitton stores suffered from low employee morale. With over a dozen stores throughout Korea and numerous department store boutiques, management had no idea how to tackle their growing problem: an apathetic staff that felt decentralized and only a small part of a huge machine. Middle managers struggled with how to motivate employees and boost performance. I conducted workshops on creative thinking and problem solving in which I challenged employees to think of the company as their own and innovate solutions to management issues. I then designed an employee committee that worked independently of management to identify problems and find solutions for corporate and employee relations, including innovating "tips and tricks" for product knowledge and salesmanship. This, along with other team-building exercises, had an almost immediate effect on employee performance and company loyalty.

The point here is that if employees are given a voice, positive reinforcement, and recognition when the company does well, the result is reciprocal respect and loyalty that goes a long way towards building a solid brand. In short, employees believe in a company that believes in them.

Chapter 13: The Take-Away

Customer service continues to be arguably the most critical factor in determining the success of a store. The store employee essentially "seals the deal" and brings the brand's core values to life. A store like Nordstrom has a reputation for building strong employee loyalty as well as the loyalty of customers.

Customer-centric companies are proven to be 60 percent more profitable than those that are not. The hospitality industry invests considerable time and expense into ensuring that employees are the perfect embodiments of the brand and that they take ownership of the customer experience. In turn, they are given positive reinforcement and reward in the form of recognition and empowerment in being part of the company's success. Together these are the secrets of a store that is dedicated to both employee and customer satisfaction.

CHAPTER FOURTEEN
The Ten Commandments of a Great Men's Store

There are no exceptions. To create the ideal men's retail experience, one must invest in a foundation of goods and services that make the total experience meaningful and authentic. Throughout this book, I have explored in detail the factors for success with a broad spectrum of environments. The following are the Ten Commandments of a Great Men's Store.

1) **Get the Goods—and Believe in Them.**

   Maintain a sharply focused selection of merchandise that is tailored to your target market and communicates your point of view. Display it well, stock it well, and make sure everyone knows you have it.

2) **Make Service a Priority, and Never Compromise.**

   Next to product, the people in the store are the faces of your brand. Make sure they're people who love what they do and do it well. Apple doesn't hire just anybody to work in their store and neither should you. The sales associates should be mentors and friends to the men who shop there and should guide them through every phase of their sartorial search for self.

3) Give Them Something They Can't Find Anywhere Else.

Make a visit to your store a unique experience where they customers can discover something they've never seen before. Park the latest concept car in the middle of the store. Feature live, acoustic concerts. Brew your own beer.

4) Selling Isn't the Only Goal; Make Time to Connect.

Retailing is about relationships. Make time to connect with your customers in unconventional ways. Host a beer night at a neighborhood bar. Call customers when their favorite brands arrive in store. Stay connected through your Web site. Partner with a volunteer organization. Support customers' social causes.

5) Keep It Real.

The best men's stores are the ones that don't seem to be trying. They have comfortable chairs, beers on ice, and the TV tuned to football. Set up some chairs on the sidewalk. Host a backyard barbecue. Give their dogs a reason to stop by, too, by keeping dog treats by the door.

6) Give 'Em Room—Especially in the Fitting Room.

Two things generally overlooked in retail design are stockroom space and fitting rooms. A great fitting room should be large enough for two and well ventilated. Halogens heat up the room, so make sure it's cool in there. If possible, have a TV just outside the door so he can keep track of the game.

7) Tell Them Something They Didn't Already Know.

Make the store into more than a store. Offer free workshops on investing, or a chance to learn about collecting wine. Invite authors and artists to discuss their work.

8) Create a Great Community and Evolve the Idea of a "Third Place."

Starbucks may have a monopoly on Oldenberg's thesis (see chapter 5), but it's become a tired concept that doesn't really bring people together. Expand the spectrum of interactive opportunities your store can offer. Organize a baseball team made up of customers and store staff. Offer seasonal ski trips. Create business-networking parties. Give men a meaningful community, not just another WiFi-enabled coffee shop.

9) Make Them Feel Like Hugh Hefner.

Hire attractive saleswomen. Host social mixers where men and women can meet each other. Take them back to the 1950s with a burlesque show.

10) Show and Tell a Great Story.

Use visual merchandising to its best advantage and by telling a compelling story with displays. Mannequins are critical to illustrating how looks work together. Make sure that store staff are well versed in the brands you carry and that they can accurately communicate the important features and benefits of the products.

CONCLUSION

Branding the Man: Retailing's Next Frontier

Readers who have followed the argument of this book will have already correctly guessed my conclusion. I believe that successful retailing to men has at its core a deep understanding of male buyers' psychology. By this I mean that retailers must have the ability to put themselves imaginatively in their customers' place, as well as a firm belief in their own brand's meaning and message, rather than desperately following in the wake of the next big thing.

The corollary is that one must respect the customer for who he is, and intuit what he wishes to become. A brand has to speak to the needs (conscious or not) that men have for self-evolution. A man will buy if he believes that his purchase will contribute to his well-being, which can be interpreted as success in business, the search for and conquest of love, or simply confidence and comfort in who he is. He may achieve this through the silent language of an expensive watch, an exclusive brand of fragrance, or an impeccably tailored sport coat. But it is the store and the branded experience that imbues these things with the magic and meaning that make a believer out of the man.

Where will he go to buy, and what will help him make the purchase he truly wants? If this book has devoted considerable space to brand positioning, it is because I believe that this is key in men's retailing. It isn't hard to find examples of brands that have chosen not to invest in a well-planned strategy, or have only done a minimal amount of long-term planning.

A great men's store has a rich authenticity, from the "big idea," to the merchandise assortment, to the store's scope of services. I've explored the experience of shopping in a thoughtfully planned shopping environment, and here I've shown that it can be transformative. In order to make that transformation happen, a retailer must tell a compelling "story" by means of the store, its atmosphere, its staff, and the brands it sells.

Ralph Lauren is, of course, the textbook example of a brand that is rich with undertones and overtones: the story of a man and his fantasy of an American aristocracy. Just as he recreated himself, he has given people everywhere the opportunity to recreate themselves. Through the magic of his story and his story telling, the former Ralph Lifshitz has not only built a castle, but has invited the public to share its romantic glamour. Mr. And Mrs. Everybody can purchase country squire clothing and imagine themselves inhabiting a world of chintz and croquet, martinis and polo: a world of easy elegance that is distinctly "to the manor born."

To be sure, the importance of strategic planning and cunning marketing in creating a great menswear retail brand cannot be overstated: the Lauren brand is not built on fantasies, but on a calculated set of strategies. However, as I hope to have shown, other ingredients, such as imagery, value, and emotional connection with the customer, have equal importance.

The longevity of a retail brand depends as much on its relevance to a man's life (or the life he aspires to) as it does on innovation, novelty, and skilled marketing.

Men are less susceptible to and more skeptical of marketing than women, but once they believe in a brand, they can be profoundly loyal. A marriage of substance and style makes for a winning brand with heart and soul that are irresistible. When linked to consistency in standards and practices, it has the potential to go on forever.

Menswear is truly the next frontier of retailing. But to brand the man, one must understand who he is and who he wishes to become. Men dream of power, success, and dominance. They want to meet society's definition of manhood in a world where all such definitions have become fluid and slippery. They sometimes even turn to magazines, television, and Hollywood for guidance. But they are also keenly aware of each other, and they measure themselves against the other men around them. Masculinity (and its meaning) is, at times, an ad hoc construct that remains aloft by virtue of the men who believe in its existence. "Masculinity," writes sociologist Michael Kimmel, "is a homosocial experience, performed for—and judged by—other men."[1] Men are constantly presented with a menu of behavioral and aesthetic examples from which to choose, depending on their ambitions and their social status. Among these examples are styles of dress that clearly delineate the personas they wish to present to the public.

A man in search of himself who seeks to emulate a certain sartorial style (and be perceived as a certain kind of person) will look for a store that understands him on more than a superficial level. This is where a superior retail experience comes in. It will satisfy his immediate need but also gradually and tactfully help him to recognize his quest for evolution and burnish his image with a foundation that offers not just great merchandise, but also a point of view that speaks to who he is and who he can become.

Appendix I

Men's Apparel Sales (By Category)

April, 2009. Courtesy NPD Group

The following charts offer a snapshot of the year-to-year increase in men's category sales, and the corresponding dollar values. Menswear, while equally affected by economic instability as any other retail category, remained relatively stable in 2008. The performance of categories like men's tailoring and outerwear suggested that men are investing in solid foundation pieces.

But the growing unemployment and corporate downsizing of the fourth quarter of 2008 and early 2009 pounded overall sales of even tried-and-true basics. All categories were affected with negative dollar percentage change, but stable in regards to percentage of dollar volume.

In the long term, suiting and tailored clothing show continued potential to rebound as the economy recovers and men face the challenge of an increasingly competitive job market. As men evolve and grow in their self-awareness and interest in fashion, other categories (such as accessories) will build in significance.

Dollar Volume (%) May–Apr 2009

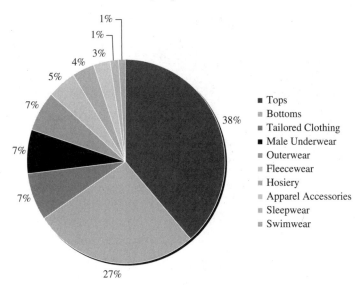

Dollar Volume (%) May–Apr 2008

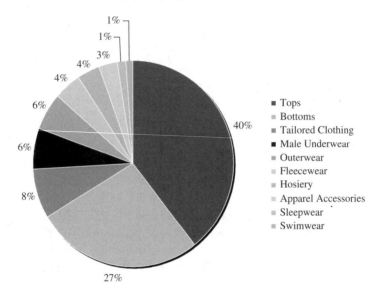

Dollar Volume (%) May–Apr 2007

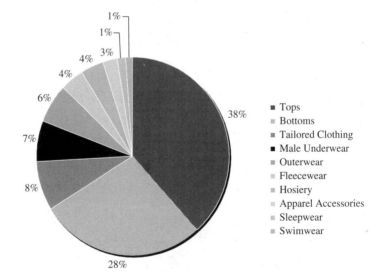

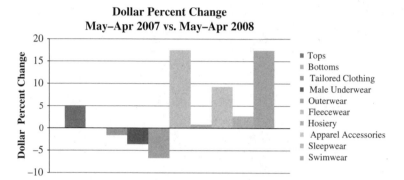

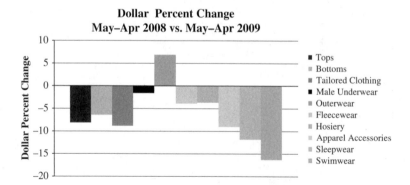

Appendix II

HOMME: A Menswear Retail Model

The following is a brand identity plan for a hypothetical men's store. In very simple branding terms, it breaks down the defining characteristics and strategies for a men's retail store concept. Those looking to start a men's business or update an existing one will find it useful as a branding exercise of key features and programs.

Most of the store's features and characteristics could be applied to virtually any store, large or small. All of them have a practical foundation in demonstrating the overarching brand concept of an ideal men's environment.

With each of the proposed features and design elements, one must, of course, consider the costs and benefits involved. But as I've argued in this book, through a combination of business strategy and design innovation, it is possible for any store to deliver a memorable experience that has both integrity and authenticity, and that resonates with a male demographic.

This store, which I've named HOMME, is hypothetically located in a medium to large-sized city in order to best serve an upwardly mobile demographic. The merchandising philosophy is precisely what I have emphasized, as are the customer service signatures.

Section 1: Brand Positioning

1.1 Mission Statement

HOMME will provide upwardly mobile, professional men, with an alternative to major retailers in regard to overall philosophy, merchandise assortment, customer service, and special in-store components, with the ultimate goal being to make shopping an entertaining and inspiring experience.

1.2 Business Philosophy

An Unfulfilled Men's Retail Need

Most menswear departments, and even some specialty stores, follow a tried and true formula for retailing to men. HOMME will offer a unique "men's club" in which men can find everything from suits to casual basics in an environment that makes HOMME an inspiring destination and satisfies men's fashion and lifestyle interests.

Our Goal: To Liberate and Educate Ordinary Men

We believe that men seek to evolve their self-image. They are wary of new ways of dressing and desire a trustworthy personal guide in this self-transformation. If "the clothes make the man," then HOMME has the power to transform them via a stellar clothing assortment and in-store components such as an inspiring exhibition space, a seductive bar and lounge, and a barbershop with discreet grooming services. Together, these will make HOMME an important part of a man's life in virtually every way, both personally and professionally.

More Than A Store: A Community Nexus for Men and the Women Who Love Them

HOMME is as much clothing store as a place to meet friends, make friends, and discover why the world wouldn't be the same without testosterone. It's a place to get the goods and at the same time, be inspired by art exhibits, music, travel, grooming, and a decent cocktail with some cool guys and attractive girls. Our mantra: Why buy it there when you can get it here, and have fun doing it?

1.3 Market Advantage

HOMME is a unique concept that challenges the norm in menswear retailing and offers a bold set of goods and services in an authentic environment. To properly satisfy the young, upwardly mobile male customer, one must understand the psychology and sociology of the evolving man. We understand both and have applied our research to developing a strategic plan for targeting this particular male customer. We believe HOMME has the ability to tap into the often ignored and generalized retail market known as the American male. This evolving

customer is in need of a more sophisticated place in which to shop, and HOMME will fulfill that need.
Our expertise includes:

Strategic Knowledge

A broad assembly of research and data on current menswear retailing strategies in local, national, and international cities, and the ability to apply this research and data to the U.S. market.

Marketing Knowledge

Trend-forecasting, e-tailing, social networking, and event concept strategies, as well as a broad base of multimedia and multichannel retail strategies.

Proven Experience

Our C.E.O. and management team are retail professionals with extensive experience in brand building for luxury brands, hospitality environments, and the entertainment industry, both in the U.S. and abroad.

Retail Philosophy

Our philosophy is built around providing a carefully edited selection of merchandise designed to adapt itself to our target customer's real-life needs. We will feature the best from the world's top established and emerging designers, as well as classics that have stood the test of time.

1.4 Value Proposition

A Practical and Entertaining Retail Environment

HOMME will serve to satisfy basic wardrobe needs and offer a truly unique environment in which men can shop and ultimately be entertained and educated. Our apparel offerings will be real clothes that real men want to wear. Our customer service and tandem goods and services will satisfy the other needs this male customer has for camaraderie, confidence, and personal growth.

HOMME will accomplish this via the following:

1) Merchandise Assortment
   A category mix of apparel that takes into account men's actual needs and desires regarding their appearance, while offering the choice between classic and luxury brands.

2) *Social Environment*
A social area in the form of a bar and lounge, as well as curated exhibitions on technology, cars, and other cultural interests.

3) *Special Services*
A barbershop featuring special grooming services, lounging "pods," a concierge service, laundry and dry cleaning center, and travel bureau.

4) *Special Events*
HOMME events are designed to stimulate, educate, and join together the retail and community programming of the store. Events will highlight current retail offerings as well as serve to enhance the store experience and store value for the target customer.

1.5 Audience Profile

The Evolving American Male

This is an economic and social sector of men recently described as "metrosexual," but it is expanding to include a growing number of professional men in upwardly mobile geographic areas such as U.S. urban cities.

These men are looking to create a more stylish—even sexy—identity via their wardrobes. They seek to shop in places that are comfortable and relatively unpretentious. They are looking for added value to their shopping experience: shopping as entertainment.

They have recently come to understand that "fashion" and "style" can mean more than the same old khakis and polos. Thanks to the mass media and their girlfriends, they have become increasingly aware of new designers and ways of dressing. More than ever, they accept some of the newer innovations in classic designs, from jeans, T-shirts, and other sportswear, to tailored suits.

They are men who work hard and play hard. After work, they might go to a local sports bar or meet a friend for coffee. They're aware of new clubs and bars, and have recently begun to "dress up" when they go out.

1.6 Competitive Analysis

Competitive Advantage

HOMME will offer a realistic and practical range of clothing that still manages to offer a fashionable alternative to both "high" and "mainstream" fashion outlets. In addition, our customer service will reflect the true needs of the customer via intelligent and friendly female employees.

A critical factor in HOMME's competitive advantage is its offer of a destination for men beyond simply a clothing store, HOMME's services such as image consultants, a barbershop, a lounge, and bar are just some of the ways this is demonstrated.

HOMME'S primary competition is:

(1) fine menswear sellers such as Neiman Marcus
(2) luxury retailers such as Gucci, Prada, and Armani
(3) specialty stores such as Barneys New York, Jeffrey, and Louis Boston

Their Advantage

Their advantages are primarily in the realm of assortment. They each offer the quality and product range associated with high-fashion goods. Specialty retailers offer additional special services such as custom ordering, tailoring, and on-site grooming services. Most of these stores work hard to offer top-level customer service.

HOMME's Advantage Over Major Retailers: Real Clothes for Real Men

HOMME's clothing assortment is about practicality and stylishness, with little to no emphasis on designer or price; rather, the offering is defined by an individual's lifestyle and personal character.

HOMME's Advantage Over Luxury Retailers: Practical and Stylish

Luxury retailers are forced to follow the dictates of the house designer or creative director. This means that by and large, clothes emphasize a dictated "look." HOMME will offer a carefully edited collection of goods that are realistic, innovative, and never beholden to any one designer or style.

HOMME's Advantage Over Specialty Retailers: Customized Service

Specialty retailers are often too fashion-forward, offering merchandise that is impractical for more mainstream lifestyles. HOMME is about creating a customized look for each customer and helping them build an individualized wardrobe that takes into account who they are and how they live.

1.7 Opportunities and Threats

The perceived threats to our business concept represent some remarkable opportunities, ones that only solidify the HOMME brand. The following are just a few examples.

Competitive Leadership: A Leader in the Retail Community

HOMME's competition offers a unique opportunity to work alongside others in the menswear business and championing of the "best in menswear."

Our competition will come to depend on HOMME as a retail think tank. HOMME will act as a sounding board for new products and service strategies that they might eventually adopt into their own merchandise assortment.

Our strong involvement in the area of the arts and entertainment will make us an important part of the community. In time, HOMME will become a recognized corporate citizen, encouraging community stewardship and responsibility — not simply retail enterprise.

1.8 Brand Architecture

Optimum Goods and Services for Men

Our store will feature the best brands regardless of price point, based on quality distinction. Our customer service will generate trust in our expertise and help us develop long-term relationships with our customers.

An Entertaining Retail Environment

In addition, we will offer the services and entertainment in an authentic and relaxed environment. Our sports bar and evening club, barbershop, and special events will provide customers with the camaraderie they crave—in a place where "everybody knows your name." As our business grows, these components will become valuable business ventures that will stand on their own.

Retail Innovation and Customer Satisfaction

HOMME will become the business model for the future of menswear retailing, using innovative concepts and techniques with which to grow the male customer.

Community Leader

HOMME will become a model and leader for retailing and develop strategic partnerships with other retail stores.

Section 2 Marketing Strategy

2.1 Market Characterization

Price: Optimum Value

HOMME will provide a realistic and practical offering of clothes that enhance a man's lifestyle. Our defining principles are value and quality, regardless of price. Our product range could include a three-pack of Hanes underwear for $15, a $45 pair of jeans, and a $1,500 designer jacket.

Product Quality: Integrity and Style

Our product assortment is all about common-sense merchandise that is based more on its integrity in a man's wardrobe than it is on status. We believe most "regular guys" want clothes that aren't high-concept, but aren't boring either. Style, function, and quality are integral to their fashion needs.

Physical Quality: Titillating

HOMME will consistently titillate and take our customer by surprise. Shopping in our store is as much about the overall atmosphere as it is about the clothes. HOMME's goal is to be a constant surprise. Each time the customer comes in there will be an element of surprise, created with exhibits, entertainment, special guests, and much more. Our goal is to bring shopping to a level of entertainment.

Speed: Evolutionary

HOMME's goal is to remain adaptable to the actual needs of men. Men are increasingly expected to "dress to impress" in both the professional and personal spheres. But men still want it to be easy and practical. HOMME will always keep this in mind. Shopping will be made easy via a clear system of merchandising and our sales staff and consultants. HOMME will be easy in and out, while encouraging the customer to stay and enjoy the overall environment of the store.

2.2 Brand Personality

Practical + Fun

HOMME will provide an unusual assortment of clothing that is all based on the basics that every man has and wants in his wardrobe, but with a fashion-forward quality that gives these garments a twist on the classics. HOMME will accomplish this in an environment that playfully provokes, entertains, and inspires our customer.

Charismatic

HOMME will inspire, titillate, and entertain our customer all at once via its unique personality. Part of HOMME's appeal will be its fun and friendly mix of consultants and sales staff, who will develop strong relationships with their clients and make them feel at home at HOMME. Our special events, social mixers, and co-sponsored spectacles will similarly engage our customer.

Wide Reaching

The physical environment will be more than just a selling space. It is a social environment where men can meet friends, experience new technology, or take in an art exhibit. The indirect store components of gallery and exhibit space, bar and lounge, barber shop, and concierge service is about making HOMME a destination for men and an extension of their lives. Each visit to the store will be a new and exciting experience. The customer will come there because it makes him feel intelligent, sophisticated, and stylish.

2.3 Business Statement

Market Need: A Unique Menswear Shopping Experience

Most menswear departments and specialty stores follow the tried and true formula of retailing, which essentially hasn't changed in 100 years. HOMME will offer a highly unusual environment in which men can find everything from suits to casual basics, in an environment that feels like hanging out at the Playboy Mansion.

Solution: HOMME, Because "All Work and No Play Makes Jack a Dull Boy"

HOMME is as much a clothing store as a place to meet friends, make friends, and discover the essence of who we really are, and can be. It's a place to get the goods, and be inspired by art exhibits, music, travel, grooming, and a cocktail with some cool guys and attractive girls.

Philosophy: You're Right at Homme

This environment is as much about the clothes as the lifestyle that goes with it, including sports paraphernalia, the latest in technology gadgets, a travel bureau, barbershop, and sports-inspired bar. It's about meeting people that make you feel welcome in an environment that could become your second...home.

2.4 Offering Statement

Offering Overview: From Everyman to The Man

At HOMME, a man can find the clothes that make the man, from the perfect pair of jeans to the perfect jacket; the goods that transform him from Everyman to The Man. It's a place that makes shopping more than a means to an end, but actually entertains him and inspires him to try new things, explore himself, and meet new people.

How We Work: Selection, Service & Satisfaction

At HOMME, a customer receives the Pygmalion experience, the chance to become all that he's ever wanted to be. We offer goods and services that help him discover his real self.

Selection

Our carefully edited assortment of merchandise will give men the authentic clothes they've been looking for; the "best of the best" in menswear, whether it is budget or luxury priced.

Service

Our customer service is based on the model often used with personal stylists and fashion consultants. Our consultants will develop close personal relationships with their clients and work with them in building the perfect wardrobe that fits their lifestyle needs.

Satisfaction

HOMME will become a destination for men in much the same way that a gentlemen's club was a destination for men in bygone times. Here they can relax in our bar and lounge, see an exhibit in our gallery, interact with the latest technology and transportation engineering (automobile prototypes will often be on exhibit), get a haircut or facial in our barbershop, and meet friends—or encounter women who will visit our store for the chance to meet an eligible man.

2.5 Pricing Statement

Pricing Overview

Good clothing is about quality and integrity, not simply the status that is so often attributed to high-priced merchandise. At HOMME, we believe that a perfect pair of $35 Levi's jeans can be paired with a $1,500 Prada jacket. Therefore, our selection will range from $15 BVD or Fruit of the Loom underwear to a Gucci suit for $2,000.

2.6 Management and Staffing

A Marriage of Hospitality and Retail

The key people involved in the operations and maintenance of HOMME are an important combination of individuals from the hospitality industry and retail. Retail professionals will be enlisted based on their ability to create innovative approaches to building a service-oriented store using alternative selling techniques, merchandising, indirect marketing and co-branding strategies, and developing HOMME into a model for the future of retail enterprise.

C.E.O.

The C.E.O. will be a dynamic individual who has a broad background in the entertainment, hospitality, and/or retail fields. She or he will set the tone for the overall operations and talent who fill the critical roles in decision making for their individual responsibilities. In addition, they will be instrumental in keeping HOMME fresh via their knowledge of event production, media, interior design, and merchandise.

C.F.O.

The C.F.O. will have the versatility and astuteness to see all of the dimensions of the financial opportunities in a store like HOMME.

HOMME is a lifestyle store built around a men's furnishings business. The individual must have the ability to bring indirect store components into play via a careful balancing of budgets, especially in regard to marketing, co-branding and co-sponsorships, and building the company's portfolio to prepare for the brand's future as a possible chain of stores in the United States.

Board of Directors

Our Board of Directors will draw from a broad range of fashion, hospitality, and entertainment individuals who will offer their expertise in their fields as it relates to HOMME's overall image and operations. Their role will be instrumental in continuing the innovative spirit in making HOMME a destination for men.

Store Manager

The Store Manager will be the "ringleader" of HOMME, ensuring a smooth operation between each of the store's components: retail, bar and lounge, barbershop, and special events. She or he will act as a talent scout for the appropriate personalities who will represent the brand on the selling floor. They will also keep a careful eye on the balance of profit within the overall structure of HOMME.

Department Managers

Each department manager will be responsible for maintaining the integrity of their individual area: retail, bar and lounge, and barbershop. Their qualifications will include their sizable influence in the community in attracting the right audience, and maintaining the atmosphere of their department. Responsibilities include staff management and customer service.

Marketing and Publicity Manager

The marketing and publicity manager will play an instrumental role in bringing important attention to HOMME's concept. This position's focus will be on bringing events that will add value to the experience of shopping at HOMME. A large part of HOMME 's success will be dependent on the maintenance of a consistent calendar of events, spectacles, and outside sponsorships that will bring recognition (and customers) to the store.

Maître d' or Concierge

This position is much like what is found in a fine restaurant or hotel; an individual who is able to make guests feel comfortable in the environment of the store, and who can assist in satisfying their needs. We believe that acts of goodwill will help build loyalty with our customers, which is why the concierge will offer assistance in booking reservations for concerts, shows, and restaurants and give suggestions for other kinds of entertainment. He or she will have a strong pool of contacts from which to draw.

"Style Consultants" (i.e., Sales Associates)

Our sales associates will offer their wisdom and advice for how our male clientele can better his appearance. These individuals will be considerate of the customer's realistic needs, whether based on lifestyle, income, or goals. Many of the Consultants will be intelligent and charismatic females, adding energy and excitement of being at HOMME.

3.0 Brand Identity

3.1 Company Metaphors And Taglines

Brand Name Justification

"Homme" means "man" or "male" in French. It is a simple and concise way to explain a store that is dedicated to men. Even if the customer does not know the meaning of the word, it sounds firm and serious, while being elegant at the same time. The pronunciation is *om*, but when it is mispronounced, the effect is that of *home*. The double meaning is effective in connoting warmth and security.

Our unique ability is ultimately to show that "the clothes make the man," and that at HOMME, a man can discover an enhanced self, via the goods and services we provide. To a certain extent, our store provides added value via the clothes and accessories we sell.

Brand Logo

HOMME's logo is deliberately simple, with an asterisk as its only decorative element. The clean and simple font-style emphasizes the clearly defined approach our store takes to a man's appearance and lifestyle.

In-store branding will carry out the red and blue highlights, with store directory graphics designed around European freeway signage.

Slogan

"Welcome HOMME."
Our slogan is designed to clarify that HOMME is more than a menswear store; it is a destination for pleasure, and the bettering of one's self-identity, in a comfortable environment.

Endnotes

Introduction

1 John Berger, *Ways of Seeing* (New York: Penguin, 1972).

2 Holly Brubach, "Men Will Be Men," in *A Dedicated Follower of Fashion* (London: Phaidon Books, 1999), 108–113.

3 American Society for Aesthetic Plastic Surgery, "ASAPS - Press Center," www.surgery.org/press (accessed March 11, 2008).

4 Jonathan Rauch, "Buff Enough?," *Reason* (November 2000): 59–61.

5 Michael Kimmel, "Wimps, Whiners, and Weekend Warriors," in *Manhood In America* (New York: Free Press, 1997), 311.

Chapter 1: Who's The Man?

1 Arthur Schlesinger, Jr., "The Crisis of American Masculinity," *Esquire* (November, 1958).

2 Erving Goffman, *Behavior in Public Places: Notes on the Social Organization of Gatherings* (New York: The Free Press/ MacMillan, 1963).

3 H. Markus and P. Nurius, "Possible Selves," *American Psychologist* 41: 954–969.

4 Stuart Ewen, "Marketing Dreams: The Political Elements of Style," in *Consumption, Identity, and Style* (New York: Routledge, 1990).

5 H. Markus and P. Nurius, "Possible Selves," *American Psychologist* 41: 954–969.

6 Sophie Woodward, "Standing Out as One of the Crowd," in *Fashion v Sport,* ed. Ligaya Salazar (London: Victoria & Albert Museum, 2008), 67.

7 "There is more freedom today for men to be whoever they want to be," said Mary Meehan, vice president and cofounder of Iconoculture, a trend tracking agency. From an interview with the *New York Times,* March 28, 2004.

8 Thomas Cunningham, "The New New Thing," *DNR Lifestyle Monitor,* September 19, 2003.

9 WSL Strategic Retail, "Methodology: How America Shops," 2002.

10 Ibid.

11 Ibid.

12 *Men's Health,* "Meet the Men's Health Guy," http://www.menshealth.com/mediakit/aud_demos.html (accessed March 22, 2008.).

13 David Carr, "A Men's Version of *Lucky* Magazine," *New York Times,* March 7, 2003.

14 Eric Wilson, "O.K. Fellas, Let's Shop. Fellas? Fellas?," *New York Times,* April 2, 2006.

15 NPD Research, February 2008.

16 Pamela Church Gibson, "Brad Pitt and George Clooney, the Rough and the Smooth: Male Costuming in Contemporary Hollywood," in *Fashioning Film Stars: Dress, Culture, and Identity,* ed. Rachel Moseley (U.K.: British Film Institute, 2008), 62.

17 Diane Crane, *The Social Agenda of Clothing* (Chicago: University of Chicago Press, 2001), 178.

18 Warren St. John, "Metrosexuals Come Out," *New York Times,* July 22, 2003.

19 Nanette Byrnes, "Secrets of the Male Shopper," *BusinessWeek,* September 2006.

20 "Putting the Manly in Manicure," *New York Times,* July 6, 2006.

21 Robert Cribb, "A Men's Shaver That's Not for De-Tufting the Face," *Star* (Toronto), May 28, 2007.

22 Michael Specter, "I Am Fashion," *New Yorker,* September 9, 2002.

23 Ibid.

24 Michael Kimmel, *Guyland: The Perilous World Where Boys Become Men* (New York: HarperCollins, 2008).

Chapter 2: Why the Men's Store Must Change

1 Paco Underhill, *Why We Buy: The Science of Shopping* (New York: Touchstone, 2000).

2 David Coleman, "Possessed: One Man's Fancy, One Leg at a Time," *New York Times,* April 11, 2004.

3 Wilkes Bashford, in discussion with the author, August 2008.

4 Ira P. Schneiderman, "Men's Outpaces Women's," *DNR Lifestyle Monitor,* January 16, 2003.

5 Beth Carlin, "Male Call," *Retail Traffic,* August 2003.

Chapter 3: When Retail Is Relevant

1 Cotton Incorporated: Textile Consumer Study, "Internet Apparel Shoppers Resemble Specialty Store Shoppers," June 2000.

2 Durand Guion, in discussion with the author, August 2008.

3 Aaker, David. *Building Strong Brands* (New York: Free Press, 1995), 84.

4 John Ryan, "Selfridges: It's the Blob!," http://vmsd.com/content/ selfridges (January 1, 2004).

5   Rebecca Voight, "Now Housing: Dunhill's New Digs," *New York Times Style Magazine,* Fall 2008.

6   Bill Saporito, "Seduction Booths," *Time,* Spring 2003.

7   Topman, "Topman - Men's Clothing," Topman, http://www. topman.com (accessed March 9, 2006).

Chapter 4: Where the Boys Are

1   Michael Kimmel, "Wimps, Whiners, and Weekend Warriors," in *Manhood in America* (New York: Free Press, 1997), 310.

2   "Cheers," Museum of Broadcast Communications, www. museum.tv/archives/etv/C/htmlC/cheers/cheers.htm (accessed September 9, 2007).

3   A. Rose and J. Friedman, "Television Sports as Mas(s)culine Cult of Distraction," in *Out of Bounds: Sports, Media and the Politics of Identity* (Bloomington, Indiana: Indiana University Press, 1997), 3.

4   Green's Sports Bar customers, in discussion with the author, June 2008.

5   James B. Twitchell, *Where Men Hide* (New York: Columbia University Press, 2006).

6   Charles Passy, "Shopping for a TV—and Staying Sane," *Wall Street Journal,* September 4, 2008.

7   James Bickers, "Breaking the Rules of Retail," *Retail Experience,* January 2008.

8   Marshal Cohen, in discussion with the author, June 2008.

9   Katherine Frank, *G-Strings and Sympathy: Strip Club Regulars and Male Desire* (Durham, N.C.: Duke University Press, 2002), 242.

10 James B. Twitchell, "Strip Clubs: Hiding Behind the Ogle," in *Where Men Hide* (New York: Columbia University Press, 2006), 160.

11 Hungry I customers, in discussion with the author, June 2008.

12 Thomas Beller, "What I Learned at the Strip Club," *Men's Health*, June 2008.

13 Van Den Bergh, DeWitte, and Warlop. "Bikinis Instigate Generalized Impatience in Intertemporal Choice," Katholieke Universiteit Leuven, Faculty of Economics and Applied Economics, in *Journal of Consumer Research*, September 10, 2007.

14 Ibid.

15 Virginia Postrel, *The Substance of Style* (New York: HarperCollins, 2003), 62.

16 Michael Kimmel, "Playing for Keeps," in *Manhood in America* (New York: Free Press, 1997), 127.

17 Michael Kimmel, "Wimps, Whiners, and Weekend Warriors," in *Manhood in America* (New York: Free Press, 1997), 310.

Chapter 5: Where Men Are King

1 Elisabeth Badinter, *XY: On Masculine Identity* (New York: Columbia University Press, 1997), 76.

2 Ray Oldenberg, *The Great Good Place* (New York: Marlow & Company, 1991).

3 Kit Yarrow, in discussion with the author, August 2008.

4 Ibid.

5 Ibid.

6 Ibid.

Chapter 6: Creating the Branded Men's Environment

1   John O'Shaughnessy, *The Marketing Power of Emotion* (Oxford University Press, 2002), 181.

2   Alina Wheeler, *Designing Brand Identity* (Hoboken, N.J.: Wiley, 2006), 26.

3   Sophie Woodward, "Standing Out as One of the Crowd," in *Fashion v Sport*, ed. Ligaya Salazar (London: Victoria & Albert Museum, 2008).

4   Richard Gliss, Retail analyst, Deloitte and Touche. Los Angeles. March 5, 2004.

5   Thomas J. Ryan, "Seven Resolutions for the Men's Industry," *DNR Lifestyle Monitor,* January 16, 2003.

6   "Indestructable Denim: New Fits and Finishes Drives Men's Market," *DNR Lifestyle Monitor,* June 2002.

7   Sophie Woodward, "Standing Out as One of the Crowd," in *Fashion v Sport*, ed. Ligaya Salazar (London: Victoria & Albert Museum, 2008).

8   Thomas J. Ryan, "Seven Resolutions for the Men's Industry," *DNR Lifestyle Monitor,* January 16, 2003.

9   "A Matter of Quality: Men Equate Natural Fibers with Better Apparel," *DNR Lifestyle Monitor,* December 2001.

10   *DNR Lifestyle Monitor,* June 2002.

11   Wilkes Bashford, in discussion with the author, August 2008.

12   "Rob," San Francisco, interviewed August 17, 2008.

13   Thomas J. Ryan, "Seven Resolutions for the Men's Industry," *DNR Lifestyle Monitor,* January 16, 2003.

14   David Coleman, "What's New in Suits? Look Closely," *New York Times,* April 11, 2004.

15   Tracie Rozhan, "Men Ask: Who Needs to Buy Clothes," *New York Times,* June 8, 2003.

16   Thomas J. Ryan, "Seven Solutions for the Men's Industry," *DNR Lifestyle Monitor*, January 16, 2003.

17   David Pilnick, in discussion with the author, August 2008.

Chapter 7: Retailers Making Their Mark: Who Leads? Who Follows?

1   Wilkes Bashford, in discussion with the author, August 2008.

2   David Pilnick, in discussion with the author, August 2008.

3   Lisa T. Cullen, "Have It Your Way," *Time*, December 22, 2002.

4   David Coleman, "What's New in Suits? Look Closely," *New York Times*, April 11, 2004.

5   Ken Lombardi, in discussion with the author, July 2008.

6   Maz Hattori, in discussion with the author, August 2008.

7   John MacDowell, in discussion with the author, August 2008.

8   "John Varvatos Adds Stylish Rock Appeal to San Francisco," *Oakland Tribune*, June 25, 2008.

9   Todd Snyder, in discussion with the author, August 2008.

10   John Brodie, "King of Cool," *Fortune*, September 1, 2008.

Chapter 8: Getting the Goods: Let the Merchandise Tell the Story

1   "Quality in Clothing:Does It Matter and Will Consumers Pay More for It?" http://www.cottoninc.com/TextileConsumer/ TextileConsumerVolume30 (accessed April 17, 2007).

2   NPD Research Group, 2006.

3   David Lipke, "The Greening of Men's Wear," *DNR Lifestyle Monitor*, October 9, 2006.

4   Ross Tucker, "Green Expo Touts Eco-Advantage," *WWD*, September 23, 2008.

5   Durand Guion, in discussion with the author, July 2008.

6   "Quality in Clothing:Does It Matter and Will Consumers Pay More for It?" http://www.cottoninc.com/TextileConsumer/ TextileConsumerVolume30 (accessed April 17, 2007).

Chapter 9: The Power of Retail Design

1   Craig Kellogg, "Is there a D/R in the House," *New York Times* (Home Design Supplement), Fall 2003.

2   Ibid.

3   Ibid.

4   Moss, "Moss," Moss, www.mossonline.com (accessed May 2, 2008).

5   Cathy Horyn, "A Store Made for Right Now: You Shop Until It's Dropped," *New York Times,* February 17, 2004.

6   B. Saporito, "Seduction Booths," *Time* (Fashion Supplement), Spring 2003.

7   Cathy Horyn, "Changing of the Guard at Gucci and Laurent," *New York Times,* March 12, 2004.

8   B. Saporito, "Seduction Booths," *Time* (Fashion Supplement), Spring 2003.

9   Paul Miller, "Location, Location, Location," www.multichannelmerchant.com (accessed July 17, 2008).

Chapter 10: Using Technology to Enhance the Men's Retail Experience

1   Jeanine Poggi, "Dressing Rooms of the Future," http:// www.forbes.com/style/2008/07/22/style-shopping-retailer-forbeslife-cx_jp_0722style.html (accessed July, 22, 2008).

2   Erin White, "Look Up for New Products in Aisle 5," *Wall Street Journal,* March 23, 2004.

3   Ibid.

4   "Men are more at ease online and spend more freely than women, survey says," www.InternetRetailer.com (accessed August 26, 2008).

5   Andrew Hargadon, in discussion with the author, June 2008.

6   Reena Jana, "MySpace's New Chic Clique," *BusinessWeek,* August 27, 2007.

7   Cate Corcoran, "Etailing Booms in Tough Economy." *WWD,* September 19, 2007.

8   IBM Corporation, "Moosejaw Mountaineering Reaches New Heights," http://www-01.ibm.com/industries/us/detail/resource/B648644M38541M92.html (accessed June 24, 2008).

Chapter 12: The Store as Town Square: A Toolbox for Creating Customer Community

1   Marc Gobé, *Citizen Brand* (New York, Allworth Press, 2002), 85.

2   Dean Iwata, in discussion with the author, May 2008.

3   Marianne Wilson, "New Borders Concept," *Chain Store Age,* April 2008.

4   "U.S. Dating Services Market," MarketData Enterprises, Inc., April 2006.

5   Letters to the Editor, *Wall Street Journal,* March 23, 2004.

Chapter 13: Customer Service: A Store's Recipe for Success

1   David Lipke, "Men's Shopping Magazine Set for Debut," *DNR Lifestyle Monitor,* March 1, 2004.

2   John O'Shaughnessy and Nicholas J. O'Shaughnessy, *The Marketing Power of Emotion* (Oxford University Press, 2002), 181.

3   James Bickers, "Breaking the Rules of Retail,"*Retail Customer Experience Magazine,* January 2008.

4   Tracie Rozhon, "High Fashion from Door to the Top Floor," *New York Times,* July 31, 2003.

5   Deloitte Consulting and Deloitte and Touche, *Making Customer Loyalty Real: A Global Manufacturing Study,* 1999.

6   Marc Gobé, *Citizen Brand* (New York, Allworth Press, 2002), 85.

7   Wilkes Bashford, in discussion with the author, August 2008.

8   Paul Fitzpatrick, in discussion with the author, March 2004.

9   Perry Garfinkel, "A Hotel's Secret: Treat the Guests Like Guests," *New York Times,* Saturday, August 23, 2008.

Conclusion

1   Michael Kimmel, *Guyland: The Perilous World Where Boys Become Men* (New York: HarperCollins, 2008).

Bibliography

Aaker, David A., and Erich Joachimsthaler. *Brand Leadership.*
New York: The Free Press, 2000.

Aaker, David A. *Building Strong Brands.* New York: The Free Press, 1996.

Badinter, Elisabeth. *XY: On Masculine Identity.* New York: Columbia
University Press, 1995.

Baker, Aaron, and Todd Boyd. *Out of Bounds: Sports, Media, and the
Politics of Identity.* Bloomington, IN: Indiana University Press, 1997.

Berger, John. *Ways of Seeing.* London: British Broadcasting Corporation
and Penguin, 1972.

Bordo, Susan. *The Male Body: A New Look at Men in Public and Private.*
New York: Farrar, Strauss, and Giroux, 1999.

Brubach, Holly. *A Dedicated Follower of Fashion.* London: Phaidon
Press, 1999.

Brehm, Sharon S., and Saul M. Kassin. *Social Psychology.* New York:
Houghton Mifflin Company, 1996.

Ewen, Stuart. "Marketing Dreams: The Political Elements of Style,"
in *Consumption, Identity, and Style,* edited by Alan Tomlinson. New York:
Routledge, 1990.

Faludi, Susan. *Stiffed: The Betrayal of the American Man.* New York:
Morrow, 1999.

Gobé, Marc. *Emotional Branding.* New York: Allworth Press, 2001.

———. *Citizen Brand.* New York: Allworth Press, 2002.

Goffman, Erving. *Behavior in Public Places: Notes on the Social Organization of Gatherings.* New York: The Free Press, 1963.

Goffman, Erving. *Gender Advertisements.* New York: Harper and Row, 1976.

Gurian, Michael. *What Could He Be Thinking? How a Man's Mind Really Works.* New York: St. Martin's Press, 2003.

Kimmel, Michael. *Guyland: The Perilous World Where Boys Become Men.* New York: Harper, 2008.

Kimmel, Michael. *Manhood in America: A Cultural History.* New York: The Free Press, 1996.

Luciano, Lynne. *Looking Good: Male Body Image in Modern America.* New York: Hill and Wang, 2001.

Martin, Richard and Harold Koda. *Jocks and Nerds: Men's Style in the Twentieth Century.* New York: Rizzoli, 1989.

Maurer, Daniel. *Brocabulary: The New Man-ifesto of Dude Talk.* New York: Collins Living, 2008.

Moseley, Rachel. *Fashioning Film Stars: Dress, Culture, Identity.* London: British Film Institute, 2005.

Oldenberg, Ray. *The Great Good Place: Cafes, Coffee Shops, Community Centers, Beauty Parlors, General Stores, Bars, Hangouts, and How They Get You Through the Day.* New York: Paragon House, 1989.

———. *The Great Good Place.* New York: Marlowe and Company, 1991.

———. *Celebrating the Third Place: Inspiring Stories About the "Great Good Places" at the Heart of Our Communities.* New York: Marlowe and Company, 2000.

Hebdige, Dick. *Subculture: The Meaning of Style.* New York: Routledge, 1979.

Pellegrin, Bertrand. "A Retail Analysis of Korea," 2003.

———. "Louis Vuitton, Korea: Employee Performance Analysis," 2003.

Postrel, Virginia. *The Substance of Style: How the Rise of Aesthetic Value is Remaking Commerce, Culture and Consciousness.* New York: HarperCollins, 2003.

Salazar, Ligaya. *Fashion V Sport.* London: Victoria and Albert Publishing, 2008.

Schultz, Howard. *Pour Your Heart Into It: How Starbucks Built a Company One Cup at a Time.* New York: Hyperion, 1997.

Schwartz, Barry. *The Paradox of Choice: Why Less is More.* New York: Ecco Publishing, 2004.

Twitchell, James B. *Where Men Hide.* New York: Columbia University Press, 2006.

Underhill, Paco. *The Call of the Mall.* New York: Simon and Schuster, 2004.

——. *Why We Buy: The Science of Shopping.* New York: Touchstone Books, 2000.

Wheeler, Alina. *Designing Brand Identity.* New Jersey: John Wiley and Sons, Inc., 2003.

Index

Books from Allworth Press

Allworth Press is an imprint of Allworth Communications, Inc. Selected titles are listed below.

Emotional Branding: The New Paradigm for Connecting Brands to People
by Marc Gobé (hardcover, 6¼ × 9¼, 352 pages, $24.95)

Citizen Brand: 10 Commandments for Transforming Brands in a Consumer Democracy
by Marc Gobé (hardcover, 5½ × 8½, 256 pages, $24.95)

Branding for Nonprofits: Developing Identity with Integrity
by DK Holland (softcover, 6 × 9, 208 pages, $19.95)

Advertising Design and Typography
by Alex W. White (hoftcover, 8¾ × 11¼, 224 pages, $50.00)

Design Management
by Brigitte Borja de Mozota (softcover, 6 × 9, 288 pages, $24.95)

Creating the Perfect Design Brief
by Peter L. Phillips (softcover, 6 × 9, 224 pages, $19.95)

Designing Effective Communications
edited by Jorge Frascara (softcover, 6 × 9, 304 pages, $24.95)

Looking Closer 5: Critical Writings on Graphic Design
edited by Michael Bierut, William Drenttel, and Steven Heller (softcover, 6¾ × 9 7/8 , 304 pages, $21.95)

Design Literacy: Understanding Graphic Design, Second Edition
by Steven Heller (softcover, 6 × 9, 464 pages, $24.95)

The Trademark Guide: The Friendly Handbook for Protecting & Profiting from Trademarks, Second Edition
by Lee Wilson (softcover, 6 × 9, 256 pages, $19.95)

To request a free catalog or order books by credit card, call 1-800-491-2808. To see our complete catalog on the World Wide Web, or to order online for a 20 percent discount, you can find us at ***www.allworth.com.***